21 HACKS to ROCK *your* LIFE

TEEN EDITION

STOP STUFFING AROUND, GET FOCUSED AND CREATE A LIFE THAT ROCKS!

CAT COLUCCIO

First published 2020 by Cat Coluccio

Produced by Indie Experts P/L, Australasia
indieexperts.com.au

Copyright © Cat Coluccio 2020

The moral right of the author to be identified as the author of this work has been asserted.

All rights reserved. Except as permitted under the *Australian Copyright Act 1968*, no part of this publication may be reproduced, stored in a retrieval system, or transmitted in any form or by any means, electronic, mechanical, photocopying, recording or otherwise, without prior written permission from the publisher. All enquiries should be made to the author.

Cover design by Maria Biaggini @ Indie Experts
Internal design by Indie Experts
Typeset in 11.5/15.5 pt Minion Pro by Post Pre-press Group, Brisbane

ISBN 978-0-6487029-3-1 (paperback)
ISBN 978-0-6487029-4-8 (epub)
ISBN 978-0-6487029-5-5 (kindle)

Disclaimer:
The material in this book is provided for information purposes only. The experiences discussed in this book may not necessarily be the same as the reader's experience. The reader should consult with his or her personal legal, financial and other advisors before utilising the information contained in this book. The author and the publisher assume no responsibility for any damages or losses incurred during or as a result of following this information.

For Jonathan & Bronte

*Thankyou for giving me the gift of being a mother,
And for keeping me on my toes in your teens.*

CONTENTS

Foreword	vii
Introduction	ix

SECTION 1: MIND HACKS — 1
- Hack #1 Visualization — 3
- Hack #2 Do Not Multitask! — 11
- Hack #3 Breathe! — 14

SECTION 2: PHYSICAL ENVIRONMENT HACKS — 23
- Hack #4 Clear the Clutter! — 25
- Hack #5 Ditch Working in Your Family Room or Kitchen! — 30
- Hack #6 Block the Noise! — 34

SECTION 3: HEALTH AND WELLBEING HACKS — 39
- Hack #7 Ditch the Snooze Button! — 41
- Hack #8 Move that Body! — 47
- Hack #9 Nourish Yourself! — 52
- Hack #10 Drink that Water! — 58

SECTION 4: TIME HACKS — 61
- Hack #11 Prioritizing to Reduce Overwhelm! — 63
- Hack #12 Map Your Wheel of Life — 68
- Hack #13 Knock Off the Hard Stuff First! — 75
- Hack #14 Use a Timer! — 81

SECTION 5: ATTITUDE HACKS — 87
- Hack #15 Find Your Cape — 89
- Hack #16 Establish Your Boundaries — 95
- Hack #17 Choose Your Mood — 101

SECTION 6: ACCELERATION HACKS — 107
- Hack #18 Create Systems — 109
- Hack #19 Create Your Dream Team — 118

SECTION 7: ACTION HACKS — 125
- Hack #20 Intentional Action — 127
- Hack #21 Start Today! — 134

A Final Word From Cat — 141
Acknowledgements — 145
About Cat Coluccio — 149
Want More Cat? — 151
Endnotes — 153
References — 155

FOREWORD

You were probably hoping that your parents would give you a gaming voucher or, at the very least, your own Netflix account – but instead, they've given you this book.

Not just any book either – a *self-development* book.

Now before you tell them how much their gift sucks and test your basketball skills by lobbing it into the nearest bin, can I ask you a few questions?

- How would you like to learn how to use your mind to help you get better at the skills you need to really rock your sport?
- How would it feel to be able to find anything you need in your room in an instant, without having to dig through piles of clothing on the floor?
- How cool would it be if you were able to get your school work done efficiently, giving you way more time to hang with your friends and way less time listening to your parents nagging you to study?

- How great would you feel if you could start making a positive difference to the world around you?

You don't have to wait until you are a certain age be it 18 or 21 or 30 or *whatever*, to start creating a life that rocks – you can start now, and this book will help by giving you 21 tips that you can begin using right away.

Just commit to reading one hack a day and following the action plan that goes along with it. You will be amazed at how your life will improve.

Who knows, you might even end up thanking your parents for giving you this book!

Cat

PS: Want some quick tips to help you get stuff done? Go to https://bit.ly/3Otips and get a FREE checklist: ***30 Tips to Help you ROCK your Productivity!***

INTRODUCTION

Do you ever feel like your life is so full on that your head spins and your stomach is in knots just like when you are on a roller coaster?

Before you even leave the house for school you've been nagged by your parents to throw your dirty clothes into the laundry basket, feed the pets, get off your computer/Gameboy/Xbox/iPad/phone, do your chores, eat your breakfast, stop fighting with your sister or brother and do your homework – which you forgot about last night when you were doing all of the other stuff.

Sure your parents are always complaining about how busy they are, how hard they work and how little you do to help – but sometimes it feels like they have forgotten how much stuff you have to deal with too.

Right?

From the teachers at school all acting like *their* subject is the most important and loading you up with assignments, to your sports coach expecting you to practice your skills and attend training four times a week, to the music teacher who tells you to practice your instrument every day then schedules band practices and performances on weekends, to your parents who want you to "help around the house more" – there doesn't seem to be any time left for you to breathe, let alone hang out with your friends.

On top of this, you are bombarded all day long with notifications from email, Instagram, Facebook, WhatsApp, Messenger, Snapchat and every other app out there.

How the heck are you meant to "rock your life" when you are scrambling to keep up? Is it any surprise that you are feeling tired and stressed out a lot of the time?

Meet Dean. Dean is an ordinary bloke in his last two years of high school. He's not quite cool enough to roll with the in-crowd, but is the kind of guy who gets on with nearly everyone. Dean enjoys kicking a soccer ball around at lunchtime with his mates, plays a mean game of *Call of Duty*, gets average marks in class and isn't too fussed about reading although he burned through the *Harry Potter* series when he was a kid.

On the surface, Dean looks like any average kid getting on with life; however, on the inside, he finds himself majorly stressed out. How is he going to graduate when he struggles to focus on his homework? He's sick of being late for school and sport practices, but can never seem to get organized in time. And don't even mention his diet – he cops enough from his sports coach about how he is not fit enough and should be eating healthier.

By the time that Dean gets in from his soccer practice

or maths tutoring after school it is nearly time for dinner, but he's usually not too hungry as he scoffed a huge bag of chips on the way home. His daily routine is to dump his gear by the door then get yelled at by his frazzled mom to put things away while she races to cook dinner because she just arrived home from work a few minutes earlier. He throws his gear onto his bedroom floor and heads to the bathroom only to find that his twin sister Emily is hogging it as usual.

Emily in the meantime is trying desperately to straighten her hair so that she doesn't get teased any more at school for her frizzy locks. An A student academically, she loves reading and playing the piano, yet struggles to balance her study and music practice with having a social life. She always feels like she is cramming at the last minute for tests, then beats herself up that she isn't good enough. She feels like she has to get high grades all the time or she is a failure. As her brother pounds at the bathroom door, Emily continues to wrestle with her hair, applying yet another de-frizzing serum from the assorted bottles littering the bathroom counter.

Dean and Emily are stressed and tired.

They are busy, but feel like mice going around and around in a wheel: running hard, but going nowhere. Life feels like a blur of homework, chores and being yelled at, and even though they know that their parents care about them and they have a nice home and food to eat, they don't feel happy a lot of the time. If anything, they feel like their lives are so full of things they *should* be doing that they have no time to do the things that they *want* to do, and they certainly don't feel like their lives rock in any way!

Sound a bit like your life?

The exciting thing is that you don't have to keep feeling like Dean and Emily. There are simple strategies you can learn and apply that will help you streamline your day, get more done and feel more in control of your life.

How good does that sound?

Imagine being able to focus well so that you can get your homework done efficiently, with time left over to enjoy the things that you want to do, like chatting to friends, gaming or enjoying your favourite hobby.

How great would it feel to do the things that you never seem to have time for, like try a new sport, play in a band or volunteer at an animal shelter?

These 21 hacks to ROCK your life are no guarantee that your life will suddenly be perfect, however, they are a great starting point to help you create the life that you want. Just reading them will change nothing, but if you decide now that you are going to take action and actually *use* each hack, I can guarantee that your life will be very different by the end of this book to what it is now.

Are you ready to hack your way to creating a life that rocks?

Read on!

"You'll never change your life until you change something you do daily. The secret of your success is found in your daily routine."

JOHN. C. MAXWELL

SECTION 1

MIND HACKS

"You have power over your mind –
not outside events. Realize this,
and you will find strength."

~ MARCUS AURELIUS

HACK #1

Visualization

Have you ever had a sports coach make you sit down and create a picture in your head of the skill that you are about attempt? You probably thought they were a bit mental at the time and that the whole exercise was all a bit weird.

Right?

You'd be wrong though as there is a stack of scientific evidence that links visualization with the ability to achieve a goal. When you do it properly, visualization can be a powerful tool that not only changes old patterns of thinking, but can affect your physical performance as well. In other words, if you can visualize or picture the thing you want to achieve clearly, you have a far greater chance of actually achieving it.

This idea of having athletes use visualization as part of their training program was put to the test with a study of national-level swimmers. Every week, the squad had to complete a 45-minute psychological skills training session as well as their regular physical training. This session included visualisation as well as relaxation, plus concentration techniques and goal setting.[1] The result? Even though nothing had changed with their physical training program, the entire squad had significant improvements in their performances and times.

The findings from this study are exciting and challenge us to ask ourselves this question: "What could I achieve if I used the same technique for the skills that I am trying to get good at?"

Another question to follow that one is, "If visualization can help me improve, how would having a positive outlook and attitude in general affect me?"

Without a positive attitude, we risk giving up on our dreams and goals as soon as our mood changes – and let's face it, our moods can change lots of times in one day! If we don't have the ability to hold a positive "super mood" that links directly to our goals, we risk chucking everything in and missing out on what we were aiming for, simply because we are having a crappy day.

Another study researched this idea by following students to see if those who wrote about and visualized becoming their best future selves developed a stronger positive outlook for the future than those who didn't. The results showed that those students who *did* the exercise of writing and visualizing what they wanted to become, ended up having more positive expectations for their future than others who didn't. Even more importantly, their positive outlook for their future was not affected or changed by passing emotions.[2] For example, even if they had a rotten day on the soccer pitch they still kept their positive expectation that they would improve and go on to do well in the sport, rather than giving up altogether.

I'm sure that part of you now wants to give visualization a go, but the other half probably thinks that it is all pretty stupid. The way to get around this is to understand what visualization actually does, and that begins with a brief look at the brain.

Your brain is bombarded daily with millions of pieces of information. Enough to make your head explode! Thankfully though, we operate on default mode 40–49% of the time, meaning that the brain automatically processes a lot of information, otherwise it would melt down with the amount of decisions it would have to deal with!

Can you imagine ever getting anything done if you had to debate the pros and cons of *if* you should clean your teeth, *why* you should clean your teeth, *which* toothbrush you should use, *why* that one is the best choice, *which* toothpaste to apply etc. every single day?

Default mode allows us to continue functioning while leaving mental space to deal with unusual or more urgent decisions. There is a downside, however.

We have an inbuilt "filter" called the Reticular Activating System (RAS), which is a group of nerves at the brain stem. The main purpose of the RAS is to filter the massive amounts of information that we encounter every minute and only let the important stuff through. This can lead to filtering only information that supports our point of view, though, which can cause what is known as confirmation bias. Think of when you decided to purchase a new model of Nike shoes. All of a sudden it seems like everyone is wearing them and there are ads saying how great they are all over the place. Your RAS is filtering information now in agreement with your decision to buy these shoes.

Now, imagine if your RAS is set to support default thinking that you are not able to improve your life? Imagine if you were finding information every day that showed you that you were correct in thinking yourself stuck and unable to do that thing you really want to do? Imagine if the only voices you heard out of all of the people you speak to were the negative ones telling you that you can never change?

Your filter is constantly doing its job of sifting out everything except the information that confirms your most private thoughts and beliefs, which is why – if you are to truly start ROCKING your life – it is time to reprogram your Reticular Activating System. You will be set up to win! You won't be fighting against yourself or wondering why you can never get a break like all of those other times when you tried but failed. This time will be very different.

Excited?

You should be.

Learning about the power of changing our thinking from the very core, beginning with changing our filter, has been life-changing for myself personally and, in turn, for the people I have worked with. Now we know how to set ourselves up for real and lasting changes – and that is powerful!

But back to visualization. This is the starting point for changing the filter in our brains, and the very first practical hack that you are going to start using. It's possibly the *most* important hack too, so make sure that you don't skip over it. Take the time to learn the steps properly, then grab your phone and program in your calendar when you are going to repeat it.

ACTION TASKS:

- Find a room where you will not be interrupted by people, pets or technology.
- Leave your phone in another room and sit yourself down somewhere comfortable.
- It's important now to close your eyes. Try to see yourself as having made the change you want to make. You might see yourself healthy and fit as you score a goal in soccer or basketball. You might see yourself at your graduation ceremony with your school certificate or degree in your hand. You create the picture that represents YOUR personal goal.
- Now, make sure that you add color to the picture. Add noise, smells and movement. Include every sense and make that picture as real as possible.
- Hold that picture in your mind for a few minutes. Ask yourself, "What am I feeling in this picture?" Allow yourself to really FEEL the emotion of having become that person. This is critical, as we also want to activate another part of your brain called the limbic system, which affects emotions and memories. I often get clients to "ground" or imprint this emotion even more powerfully by smelling an essential oil, usually a citrus scent. Smell is the primary sense associated with the limbic system, and bringing together the citrus smell and the positive feelings of achieving your goal will provide a powerful connection. Whenever you smell that citrus you will experience the positive feelings of the picture you visualized.

- As well as asking yourself how you are feeling in your visualization, I want you to use your other senses. What are you wearing? Where are you located? What noises can you hear? Can you feel anything? (For example, the wind on your face or the waves at your feet.)
- Create a mental image that is three-dimensional and makes you feel like you are *really* in that moment. Hold it as long as possible, then repeat this action at least twice a day for the next 30 days.

It will be life changing, I can guarantee you.

You will be amazed at how you start to find yourself noticing more and more information that confirms the picture that you see of yourself. You'll start to feel way more positive as your default mode isn't switched to negative any longer, but is instead set to hope and positive expectation.

Finally, I suspect that you might be thinking, "Who has time to sit around like that?" So let's change that attitude right away with some strong positive statements:

"I have ALL the time I need to complete my visualization exercise twice a day."

"I WANT to complete my visualization exercise twice a day."

"I'm EXCITED to complete my visualization exercise twice a day."

Feeling the emotions of these statements and saying them out loud is also reprogramming your RAS so that you will not be struggling to do your exercise, but will *want* to do it.

Now put this book down, find that quiet space and do it!

HACK #2

Do Not Multitask!

Have you ever watched TV while eating a snack, texting your friends and patting the dog next to you? You were multitasking, which means that you were doing many tasks at the same time. It is something that is so automatic to most of us that we don't even realize we are doing it!

It's easy feel like you are getting heaps done when you multitask. You listen to music while doing your homework and chatting to your friends on Messenger or Snapchat. You text your friends and check Instagram while you practice kicking goals in the backyard, and you even scroll through Facebook while sitting on the toilet!

There is a big problem with multi-tasking, however, and it is that even though you *feel* like you are getting lots done, the real truth is that you aren't.

That homework you were working on? You would have found that you were able to focus better, finish quicker with fewer errors and produce much better quality work if you had not been doing all of the extra things at the same time that you were working on it.

That goal-kicking you were practicing? You only took half as many kicks as you could have if you had not been stopping to text all of the time.

There is no way that you will get great grades at school or the Golden Boot award for your soccer club if you are operating at only half of your potential.

Science has proven that multitasking really does slow down your ability to complete your main task well. Every time that you are distracted by music, texts, Netflix or even your pet dog, it takes more time for your brain to go back to focusing on that assignment you are trying to write. You've just doubled the amount of time that you had to spend on your homework – and who wants to do that?

It's time to learn how to break the habit of multi-tasking – and this will take some effort as most of us are used to doing lots of things at the same time. When it is time to start our homework, we automatically turn on the TV or plug in our headphones to listen to music. When it's time to go outside and do some sports training, we grab our phones so we can check what's happening on Snapchat.

Are you ready to cut your homework time in half and learn how to focus so that you can *really* master your sport? Make sure that you follow the action steps for this hack!

ACTION TASKS:

- Let's face it, electronic devices are the main distraction for people today and it is easy to be addicted without even realising it. The first step is to turn your phone to airplane mode whenever you sit down to do your homework or go outside to train. Even better, place the phone upside down or leave it in another room so that you won't be tempted to check it until your task is done.
- Desperate to watch the next episode of the series you are following on Netflix? Make a deal with yourself that you can watch it *after* you have completed your task and not during! This way, not only will your task be completed quicker and at a better quality, you will also enjoy the show more as you'll be able to focus on it fully.
- Turn off notifications on your phone. Every time that you get a ping notifying you that you've had a message on Facebook your train of thought is broken, and you lose time and focus when you reply then try to get back into the work you are meant to be doing. Stopping all of your social media notifications will help you break the habit of multitasking and help you take back control of your time.

HACK #3

Breathe!

We talked earlier about how our brains are set to "default mode" and how this can be a good thing as it saves us the stress of having to make the same thousands of decisions every single day. Most of the time, our default is set to "survival mode," which means that our brain is always scanning for signs of danger so that it can alert the body to take whatever action is needed to survive. This action could be to freeze, to run or to fight.

Ever hear your parents moaning about how they wished that their lives had no stress? I'll bet that you have thought the same thing when it's getting close to the end of the school year and your teachers have gone overboard with assignments and exams. The thing is though – and I'm sorry to break this to you – there will *always* be some kind of stress in your life. That's the honest reality of what we all live with.

Stress can become a problem though when your "spider senses" get too sensitive and your survival-mode brain starts to kick into overdrive. The combination of whatever is stressing you, as well as your brain demanding that you run away or stand and fight means that you can start to feel overwhelmed. Your body reacts to this stress and can show all sorts of symptoms, including chest tightness and shallow breathing, which makes you dizzy. You might find that it gets hard to get to sleep. You might feel anxious and struggle to focus on anything. You end up not getting your work done, which means that you get even more stressed, so you start distracting yourself with Xbox or social media, which puts you even further behind – and the stress cycle goes around and around!

Thankfully there *is* something that you can do whenever you find yourself feeling anxious and overwhelmed, and wondering if you should just run away (*which would be really dumb, right?*) It is a simple technique that I have used for myself and with clients, and it will help you calm down your brain and body from being in survival mode so that you can re-focus on what you *should* be doing.

This technique teaches you how to control your breathing because when you are able to breath properly, you will find that your body starts to calm down from its primed "ready to fight" state and you will be able to start focusing again.

I was a professional saxophone player for many years. I started learning at 12 years old after winning a scholarship to a high school that had a special music program, and after that I traveled across Australia from my home in Perth to Sydney where I completed a four-year degree at the Conservatorium of Music.

In total, I had nine years of private saxophone lessons and possibly the most important thing that I had to learn was how to breathe properly. Being a woodwind instrument, without air there is no noise. If you don't blow hard enough and long enough, the quality of the sound is weak and you find yourself gasping for air every few seconds – exactly the same as if you suddenly decided to run a marathon with no training.

I had to learn to breathe deeply and create a strong airflow that lasted as long as possible. Just like how people train to run faster, I trained to increase the volume of air that I inhaled so that I could play longer phrases of music before needing another breath.

I'm sure that at some point in your life you have sung in a choir. Remember back to that time and think about what you did when you were told to take a deep breath before singing. Try it now. What did you do? Chances are, if you are anything like the hundreds of people I have worked with in choirs over the years, you sucked in a big breath while hitching your shoulders up to your ears. Unfortunately though, breathing in like this means that you will not have filled your lungs with nearly enough air because you will have sucked your diaphragm right up high and only filled the top portion of your lungs. Your diaphragm is the large muscle that runs under your lungs, above your stomach, and to *really* fill your lungs and slow down the rapid, shallow breathing that comes with anxiety, you need to push that diaphragm down so that your entire lungs can be filled. This means that your stomach will also expand to make room as the diaphragm pushes down.

My first ever saxophone teacher had a great way of teaching his students how to breathe correctly. He would make us lie on the floor and would place a large book on our stomachs. As we took big breaths, the book would rise. More importantly though, our shoulders didn't move at all. Whenever we forgot to breathe properly and started sucking our shoulders up when we were standing, we would have to go and lay down once more with the book to remind us how deep breathing *should* feel.

There is another teacher that I will always remember who really emphasized proper breathing, and that was an opera teacher at the Conservatorium. I can still remember her standing behind me as I sang, squeezing my rib cage with her hands and commanding me, "Open your intercostals!" The intercostal muscles are located between the ribs and expand the ribs so that your lungs can inflate properly. In her own creative way, this teacher was making her students push against her hands so that we could learn how it felt to really expand our ribcages to breathe properly. We were training our muscles the same way that someone lifts weights to train their arm muscles, and without this training we would not be able to breathe deeply enough to power our voices for performance. Most of the top singers that you listen to would have done similar exercises to increase their ability to breathe.

How does this relate to you if you don't want to be a better musician or singer, however? Your breathing has a direct impact on your mental and physical wellbeing and, with practice, is something that you can control to reduce that feeling of being overwhelmed and stressed.

Now that you know about how you should be breathing, you might be surprised at what you discover next time that you find yourself feeling like you want to run away from the world.

Check yourself: how are you breathing? If your shoulders are tensed and your breathing is shallow, you will probably be feeling anxious and jittery. Breathing like this causes stress hormone levels to get even higher and you may even start to hyperventilate (breathe really quickly), which will *really* make you feel light-headed and therefore even more stressed!

It's time to break the cycle of stress and overwhelm, and learn how to breathe your way back into the present moment so that you can calm your mind and your body and get your focus back on what you are trying to do.

ACTION TASKS:

- Find yourself a large book, lie down on your back and place it on your stomach. Take your time and practice breathing both deeply and shallowly. Concentrate on how different it feels between your lungs being only half full and completely full.
- Now stand in front of a mirror and continue to practice breathing deeply. Watch to see if you can take a deep breath without raising your shoulders. Turn side on and try to expand your stomach and ribcage with every breath. My saxophone teacher told me many years ago not to worry about trying to hold my stomach in to look slim if I wanted to make a decent noise!
- Think of times when you have felt really stressed. You might have felt tight in your throat or shoulders and found yourself breathing rapidly. Is there a pattern of "trigger" situations that cause you to feel overwhelmed? Maybe it is speaking in front of the class or taking a shot at goal on the sports field. If there is an obvious event that you can identify, take note of it and be prepared to apply your deep breathing, using your diaphragm properly, the next time that you are in that situation.
- Have you found yourself feeling really overwhelmed and stressed? Follow these steps to calm your body and mind so that you can get focused once more on what you should be doing:
  1. Step away from what is stressing you. Remove yourself from the physical location where you are

feeling stressed – even if that just means walking around the corner. If you are in class, ask to go to the bathroom so that you can grab a few minutes of privacy. Otherwise, you can still pause and apply this technique quietly at your desk.

2. Expand your ribcage, push out your stomach so your diagram can go down and take a 7-second breath in through your nose, filling your lungs. Hold for 7 seconds, then breathe out through your mouth for 7 seconds.

3. Repeat this at least 3–5 times, focusing on counting the seconds until you can feel that your stress levels have dropped and you are feeling calmer. If you can, close your eyes while you are doing this exercise so that you are not thinking about anything other than your breathing. Many people refer to this as being an exercise in "mindfulness," meaning that you are not focusing on what you *should have done* or what you *should be* doing – you are just being mindful of this present moment.

4. Think about the situation that is causing you stress. What is the very first step to getting through it? For instance, if you are feeling overwhelmed and anxious about an assignment that your teacher has just given you, what is the something small that you can do to move you towards completing it?

5. Make that first step your priority and block any other thoughts about how large or long or hard

the assignment seems. Now go back to work and focus *only* on that first task until it is completed.
6. Feeling anxious and overwhelmed again once you have completed that first step? Repeat the entire process over and over, calming your survival brain that wants to run away, until you have completed your work.

SECTION 2

PHYSICAL ENVIRONMENT HACKS

"Clearing the clutter in your physical space will go a long way toward clearing the clutter in your mind."

PETER WALSH

HACK #4
Clear the Clutter!

Are you sick of hearing your dad tell you to clean your room?

Does it bug you when your mom goes on about missing glasses and plates that she swears she saw you taking into your room but that never reappeared?

Do *you* hate it when you are running late to meet your friends but you can't find your favourite shirt and one of your socks? What about when you are trying to locate that important bit of information for your assignment that is due tomorrow and you could have sworn that it was on your desk somewhere under the pile of papers that are threatening to topple over and cover your floor?

One of the buzzwords in magazines these days is "minimalism," and there are plenty of TV shows featuring people throwing out heaps of stuff and looking happier for it. The truth is that these folks really are on to something as physical clutter or mess can actually represent the state of a person's mind. Too much mental OR physical clutter can lead to stuffing around, feeling blah and having low energy, meaning that you will struggle to do what you *should* be doing.

Researchers have found that our brain absorbs information via *all* of our senses – not just though our eyes and ears.[3] Our senses of smell, taste and touch also provide information pathways to the brain, which is both amazing and a potential problem at the same time. We can receive information in so many ways and we can also be distracted in so many ways, which means that clutter can be a real issue.

Clutter is time consuming, distracting, overwhelming, embarrassing, frustrating and wastes so much of your time. A cluttered environment and a cluttered mind is not going to help someone who wants to create a life that they love!

What does your desk look like? Is it overflowing with sticky notes, pens and broken pencils, notes from school, planners, photos, paperclips and other stationary items, gaming headsets and controls, photos, phones, iPads, laptops, chargers and accessories?

How's that working for you?

The second that you stop focusing on the assignment you are trying to write and look around, you run the risk of being overwhelmed as all of your senses respond to the clutter surrounding you. Each sense will be bombarded with data and your brain will then need to filter and sort all of this information, meaning that your mental focus on what you should be doing will break.

How does your computer look? Does it have a dozen tabs open and a desktop full of items that should be deleted or filed?

What does your smartphone look like? Are there pages and pages of apps that could be grouped into files so that you don't need to keep swiping away, wasting time searching every time that you need a certain app?

While we are at it, how is the rest of your house? Do you have a drawer in your bathroom full of out-of-date products? Do you have a wardrobe stuffed full of clothing that you grew out of three years ago? Is your bedroom floor piled high with sports gear, school books, musical instruments, gaming boxes, dirty plates and last week's clothes?

All of these situations can give you a sensory overload that affects your focus and ability to do what you need to do. Even if you have a perfectly neat and tidy desk and locker at school, coming home to a cluttered bedroom is still going to raise your stress levels and hurt your motivation.

As much as you hate to admit it – maybe Mom and Dad are on to something when they tell you to tidy your room!

ACTION TASKS:

- In a nutshell, it's time to get into gear and clear the clutter! Begin with your desk and remove everything from its surface. Create three piles: items to keep, items to donate and items to throw out. Do NOT go on to any other area until you have completed this workzone! You will feel great when it is done.
- Continue now with the rest of your room, tackling one zone at a time. The zones might be your bed, your bookcase, your floor, your wardrobe and your bedside table. Be tough with yourself! You want your room to be clear and to create the lowest sensory stimulation possible so that you can either totally relax or be able to focus on your homework with no distractions.
- Keep working in one zone at a time and make your way through other "hot-spots" where your clutter has exploded in your home and on your devices. Areas to tackle in your house might be your bathroom, your sports gear in the garage, and your games and DVD collection. With your devices, it might mean clearing your laptop desktop, sorting your bookmarks, or filing your apps into groups. Feeling overwhelmed? Set yourself a target of doing just 15 minutes a day of clutter clearing, and you will soon see a huge difference to your surroundings *and* to your mood. Donate anything that you do not regularly use and trash anything that is broken. It's time to clear that space in your home and in your head!

- Once you have de-cluttered your environment, make a commitment to yourself to recreate your clear space at the end of every day. Start this new habit with your desk and then use it with your wardrobe and your bathroom. It will should only take you around 10-15 minutes of an evening before you head to bed, and doing it will set you up for a good mood and a focused headspace for the day ahead – winning!

Now put the book down and start clearing.

HACK #5

Ditch working in your family room or kitchen!

How many times do you find yourself coming in from school, grabbing a snack and plonking yourself down in the family room or kitchen where you end up staying for the rest of the evening? Here you juggle your homework on your knee in between patting the dog, answering texts and fighting over the TV remote with your brother.

We've already talked about how multitasking is not an efficient way to work, robbing you of precious minutes each time that your brain has to change its focus due to the multiple tasks you are expecting it to do. The physical environment that you choose to work in can affect you in a similar way.

Lots of businesses now have what are called "open-plan" offices where there are lots of desks in one open room, and very few cubicles and walls. This type of office plan is considered very trendy and is supposedly helpful for communication between employees. Unfortunately though, researchers are discovering more and more that this kind of space actually does *not* help people communicate or work more effectively. In fact, it has been found that the noise levels and lack of privacy contribute to distraction, stress and demotivation! Obviously this is not the result that the employer was after.[4]

Now you might be a student, but I'm sure that you have experienced similar situations. Think about your study hall, your classroom or even your kitchen at home – wherever you sit to do your work. What is happening in those spaces? I guarantee that there is a lot more going on than people being completely focused on their work.

Is someone eating their lunch nearby? Have you noticed the smell? Is their chewing getting on your nerves? Are there people walking around? Chairs scraping the floor? Someone coughing, burping or talking nearby? People bumping you or calling out to you while you are trying to focus?

What if your assignment requires you to work as a group or interview people over the phone? Do you feel like everyone around you is listening in on your conversation? On the other hand, how awkward does it feel if you are trying to write a detailed essay about the devastation of World War II and the person at the desk opposite is having an argument with their girlfriend?

Study halls, classrooms and the busy areas of your home where you like to study can lead to the distracting sensory overload that we talked about in our previous hack. Constant noise, movement, clutter and color, smells of food, even the sensation of touch with you being bumped or slapped on the shoulder in passing, are all interruptions to your mental train of thought. Once that train is disrupted, it is hard to get it back on track and regain focus. The harder the task is that you are trying to work on, the less chance you have of completing it to a high standard if your environment is constantly working against you.

Regardless of whether you are at school or at home, parents, teachers, friends, siblings, pets and even appliances all have the ability to cause those breaks in concentration that make completing your work feel like you are wading through mud – and if you want to create a life that ROCKS, you need to find or create a physical environment that helps you instead of making things harder.

ACTION TASKS:

- Chances are you have pretty little control over the physical design of your classroom or home; however, this doesn't mean that you can't make some changes. Begin by talking to the person who is in charge (for example, your teacher or the school librarian) about the possibility of having "quiet zones" created where you can work privately with minimal distractions.
- Unable to physically change your study area? Find tools that can help you to cut down the sensory overload. A great starting point is to use noise-reducing headphones while you are working on tasks that require concentration. Your friends and family will soon learn not to interrupt you when your headphones are on!
- In regards to your home, spend a weekend setting up a private workspace that removes you from the noise and distractions of the main household. If you don't have an actual room available to create your own "office" or study area, get creative! Perhaps the conversion of a closet could provide you with a private workspace, or find a corner in your bedroom where you can work undisturbed.
- Encourage your family to leave you alone when you are in your work zone. Obviously a polite note on the door explaining that you are studying will get a better response than yelling at everyone to "shut up!"

HACK #6
Block the Noise!

Noise is something that we all live with. It's not uncommon for some people to go an entire day with Spotify, radio, TV, YouTube, Netflix or whatever blaring away in the background. Unfortunately though, noise can be a real distraction to you getting focused and getting what you need to do completed. You might think that you are one of the few people not affected by noise, but trust me, you would be amazed at how much more quickly your brain functions when it is not distracted by Beyoncé's latest song.

We talked about how noise is one of the big distractors in an open plan office, study hall, classroom or home, and the shocking thing is that researchers have discovered that when you can hear someone talking while you are trying to read or write, your focus and output drops by up to 66%! That is a huge percentage![5]

How on earth will you be able to get focused, stop stuffing around and build a life that ROCKS, doing the things that you want to do, if you are operating 66% less productively than usual?

Noise pollution is a real problem and has been linked to having higher stress hormones in the body, hearing loss and even delayed reading comprehension in children![6] Putting it plainly, even though you might not always be aware of it, sound has the potential to affect your thinking, your emotions and your behavior.[7] It can be someone else's conversation, notifications or calls on your phone, overhead airplanes, traffic noise, loud music – or indeed, *any* music. All of these sounds affect your physical body immediately. Your heart rate and rhythm reacts to noise and your nervous system is especially affected, which can lead to raised stress levels.

Noise is something that really needs to be managed if you *really* want to be focused and creating the life that you want. After all, homework can suck – why drag it out any longer than you need to get it done? It's time to cut distractions like noise!

ACTION TASKS:

- I talked about using noise-canceling headphones in Hack #5, and this is a great starting point as it helps you get the silence that you need to be able to focus on your work. In fact, I am using them right now as I write because I am in the same room as my family who are watching a movie. Make sure that you are using headphones and not ear buds, though, especially if you are listening to music. Ear buds have been associated with hearing damage due to where they sit in the ear canal, which can raise levels up to nine decibels louder. Trust me as a former professional musician who spent many years on stages standing in front of guitar amps and drum-kits, and who now suffers hearing loss – you want to protect your hearing!
- Playing music through your headphones might seem a great way to distract from environmental noise; however, it can also interfere with your brain's ability to focus and recall facts – *especially* if the music is loud, and even more so if there are lyrics. How on earth will you string the words together in an English essay if you have Eminem rapping in your ears? If you do really love music, however, an alternative is to try are binaural beats: music that researchers believe can activate specific brain systems according to which frequency pattern is used. The most popular pattern that is said to promote alertness and concentration is called the "beta pattern," set at a

frequency of 14-100Hz. A free, online sample of a beta pattern binaural beat that I often listen to when working can be found here: https://www.youtube.com/watch?v=fxB82OvGEGo

- ▶ Still struggling with noise distraction? Try an app to generate "white noise" through your headphones. White noise is a background noise like a fan running, raindrops on the roof or waves washing on the beach. There are plenty of these apps available and they help mask noises like people talking that break your concentration and prevent you doing the work that you are meant to be focusing on.

SECTION 3

HEALTH AND WELLBEING HACKS

"It is well to be up before daybreak, for such habits contribute to health, wealth, and wisdom."

~ ARISTOTLE

HACK #7
Ditch the Snooze Button!

When I worked as a personal trainer there were many times that I found myself alone at the gym at 5 am. Not because I enjoyed hanging out on my own at that time of the morning mind you, but because I had been stood-up by my client, which really sucked as I would have been happy to get another hour or two of sleep!

The thing is though, these people had booked that session time with me on purpose – mainly because it was the only time they had to fit in their exercise due to their busy schedules. If they didn't turn up for a session without letting me know in advance (like if they were sick or going away on holidays), they still had to pay for that session as I could have given it to someone else if I had known in time. You'd think that not wanting to waste their money would be a pretty motivating reason to get out of bed and get to the gym, but plenty of times it wasn't, and the most common reason people missed their sessions was that they had hit the snooze button on their alarm one too many times.

Sound familiar?

As a teenager myself, (yes, many, *many* years ago …) I also was a snooze button lover. I had one of those rickety old wind up alarm clocks that ticked so loudly that the next door neighbors could have heard it at night, and in the morning the little hammer on the top hit the two little bells so hard that I would be woken up by nearly hitting the ceiling in shock. I quickly learned how to feel for the snooze switch on the back and got pretty good at hitting it with my eyes still shut every morning. Not once or twice either, but up to seven or eight times – enough times for my parents and brothers to be yelling at me to "turn that thing off!"

I hated getting up early to take my PT sessions as I was a natural night owl, which made my early rises of 3.45 am a real challenge. In previous years when I worked as a professional musician, I actually used to get home at 3.30 in the morning after gigs and this felt way more normal for me. I managed to change my body clock though, and quickly learned that if I was to get out the door on time and be alert for my clients, the snooze button routine had to go. I discovered the same thing with my personal training clients. Those who didn't hit the snooze button were the clients who were always on time – and they were also *way* more alert than those who did.

So what makes hitting the snooze button such a big deal?

You are probably sick of your parents nagging you about the importance of getting a good night sleep. Unfortunately, as much as you might not want to admit it, they are right. Quality sleep is absolutely essential for you to be at your best – healthwise and workwise. If you are suffering from lack of sleep, your brain is going to be sluggish, your immune system will be compromised (meaning that you pick up colds and other viruses more easily), and you will generally feel like you are not functioning well.

Quite frankly, you are going to feel like crap.

Good sleep habits are essential in order for you be in peak condition so that you can create your life that *rocks*. This starts with getting up at the same time every morning, which is why hitting that snooze button can derail your entire day.

When you continually hit that snooze button, waking up yet wanting to go back to sleep, the result is an uncomfortable, drowsy and disoriented state called sleep inertia.[8] Instead of you feeling refreshed and great like you do after a deep sleep, those few minutes between each snooze alarm are confusing your body and brain, and actually causing you to feel more and more groggy. This grogginess or sleep inertia can affect you for hours afterwards and all of those goals you were intending to smash out that day will probably still be sitting there uncompleted come 5 pm.

To break the snooze button habit, it helps to use the same steps that you can use when you are trying to break other negative habits in your life:

1. You need to *decide* that you are going to change things.
2. You need to *determine* what action you are going to do instead – in this case, getting out of bed straight away.

3. You need to set up your environment to *support* this outcome.
4. You need to apply some tough-love and *self-discipline*, and push through these actions again and again until the new habit is automatic.

Before you do any of these steps though, you need to answer this question: "What do I actually want to achieve?"

If your answer is "to feel refreshed, alert and great so that I can tackle the goals and tasks that I *need* and *want* to do to help me create a life that *ROCKS*," then it is time to get serious.

Right?

Decide today that you are going to put a sleep habit into place that will support the life that you want to live.

ACTION TASKS:

To set yourself up for great sleep, you need to start by creating good habits BEFORE you even get into bed:

- Have a regular bedtime. This means that at least six out of seven nights a week you get to bed at a similar time. Try to make this before 10.30 pm as your body tends to perk up again after this time, making it harder to get to sleep. Got a late-night gaming tournament planned or a late-night party or concert to go to? Try to limit these to once a week and understand that they might throw your sleeping and waking cycles out, meaning that you need to be self-disciplined to get your routine back in place.
- Stop all screen time an hour before bed time, or at least consider using yellow lenses to block the effect of the blue light of your phone. This light has been linked to the lowering of the production of melatonin, the hormone that influences the body's rhythms.[9] Yes, Mom was right again unfortunately! That phone needs to be put on airline mode after 9 pm so that you don't receive notifications that disturb your sleep either through the pings of notifications or from their blue light.
- Sleep in a cool room. Studies have shown that in order for the body to lower its core temperature and cycle through the differing stages of sleep, your best room temperature should be around 60–67 degrees Fahrenheit (approximately 15.5–19.5 degrees Celsius). If your room is too warm, you will find that

your sleep is broken and you keep waking up as your core struggles to cool down. In my case, I have a fan or air-conditioning on all year around as it keeps me cool and provides the white noise I need to mask household noises that break my sleep.[10]
- Have complete darkness in your room. Any light, particularly the blue light of a digital clock or phone, has the ability to disrupt your sleep cycles, so turn those computers off, place your phone face down and even think about wearing an eye mask if your bedroom curtains let in too much light.

Decide today that you will no longer hit that snooze button! If it is a separate button on your clock, tape it over or disable it. Otherwise, place the alarm device on the other side of the room so that you need to actually get out of bed to go and turn it off. Once you are up, you are up! Fight that urge to get back into bed and you will be well on your way to feeling more alert and focused and *rocking* your life!

HACK #8

Move that Body!

> "Leave all the afternoon for exercise and recreation, which are as necessary as reading. I will rather say more necessary because health is worth more than learning."
>
> ~ THOMAS JEFFERSON

We all know that exercise is good for the body. It helps us stay healthy, keeps us strong, keeps us flexible, lifts our mood, positively affects our blood pressure and helps our brains work more efficiently.

So why do so many of us make every excuse under the sun to not exercise?

Despite knowing how important exercise is for our health and wellbeing, it is often the first thing we ditch when we are super busy with assignments or overwhelmed by life in general. I know that I've been guilty of not exercising at certain times in my life and I bet that you possibly have too.

I also know how good I feel when I *do* exercise regularly and trust me when I say that the difference in how I feel when I do exercise compared to when I don't is pretty significant.

If you really want to *rock* your life and operate at your best, exercise needs to become an essential part of your daily routine. Really, it's up there with sleeping well, eating well and drinking enough water. But where and how do you start if exercise is not already a regular part of your life?

Being a qualified personal trainer, I believe that strength training is the gold standard for everyone, regardless of gender or age. Women need to build muscle just as much as men do – and given our hormonal make-up, it is far harder for us to do so and far easier for us to lose muscle mass rapidly if we neglect it. Girls, if you want to have shapely arms and legs, you need to ditch the thought that resistance work will make you bulky and just start lifting weights! If you are in your early teens that means doing bodyweight exercises like squats, lunges and push-ups, and as you get older you might add weights or resistance bands into your training routines.

Working with all sorts of different people over the years has taught me that the best way to start exercising is to find something that you enjoy. Some of my clients were open and happy to join me on the weights floor, but many others needed to be eased into the routine of regular exercise. Whether it was walking or hiking, dancing or team sports, those who enjoyed what they were doing were the ones who didn't only stick to their exercise routine, but were open to trying new things as well.

No idea where to start? What do you enjoy? Dancing? Gymnastics? Team sports like soccer or basketball? Swimming? You don't need to be great to participate as most sports have lots of grades, including social grades where you can join in and enjoy regardless of how skilled you are. The key is to get moving, not aim for the Olympics. (Unless that is a goal that you are specifically aiming for!)

At the end of the day, if you can change your view of exercise from being something that you *have* to do to something that you *want* to do, you will find that half the battle is won right there. Add in the bonus of the endorphins, the "happy hormones" that are released by your body when you exercise, and you will be feeling on top of the world in no time!

ACTION TASKS:

- When you are planning your timetable for the following week, make sure that you schedule exercise into your diary along with your lessons and assignments. Treat this appointment with as much importance as any of your other ones and decide now to keep your promise to yourself that you will follow through. While some people prefer to schedule their exercise session early in the morning before their day begins, others find that their schedule works better when they plan to exercise later in the day. Find out what works for you – before classes, at lunchtime, or after school or university – and stick to it!
- Book in a personal training session, swimming lesson or a private sports-skill lesson to help you get started. One of the hardest things that people face when beginning a new exercise program or sport is the fear of the unknown. Not knowing how the machines work in the gym, what the rules are for your sport, or feeling like you will embarrass yourself by doing the wrong moves in front of others shouldn't stop you from having a go. Be proactive from the get-go by booking an appointment with a trainer or instructor who can not only help you feel more comfortable with exercising safely and effectively, but also familiarize you with the space you will be exercising in or help you understand the sport that you want to learn.

- Have your sports bag packed and ready to go the night before. Speaking from personal experience, there is nothing worse than staggering around at 3.45 am looking for a clean pair of socks! Having your sports gear sorted, packed and ready to either put on or take with you, will make sticking to your commitment to exercise so much easier. I have dozens of former clients who will tell you that this simple act, as well as not pressing that snooze button anymore, totally changed their lives in regards to exercising regularly.

HACK #9
Nourish Yourself!

Have you ever had a night where you ate all the burgers, pizza, donuts and icecream that you could fit in, then felt sluggish, bloated and blah for the next few days? Or have you been on holidays where you ate take-away for days until you found yourself craving the simple, wholesome meat and three veg that your mom cooks at home?

These days, most of us understand that what you eat affects not only how you look in a bikini or board shorts, but also how you feel, how you think and how healthy you are. Eating the right foods can help prevent certain diseases like Type-2 Diabetes and can also help keep your brain healthy, which is critical if you are going to achieve what you need to do to *rock* your life.

Unfortunately though, understanding that food can affect us is very different to knowing what foods we actually should be eating. It feels like every social media influencer is saying that their way of eating is the best, and at least every second week one of the Kardashians seems to be advertising a new diet product. Choosing what to eat has actually gotten more confusing, even though we understand so much more these days that we need to fuel our bodies with good nutritious food!

Instead of spending the rest of this book researching and comparing the pros and cons for every way of eating out there – a subject that could easily fill three or more books – let's instead focus on one way of eating that studies have shown supports good health not only in your body, but in your brain too.

The Mediterranean Diet[11] is a way of eating based on the traditional foods consumed by the people who live around the Mediterranean Sea – in particular, the Greeks and the Italians. Their diet consists largely of good fats such as olives, avocados and fish, as well as lean meats, eggs, grains, beans, vegetables and fruits. My mother in law was a very traditional Italian lady whose food was nearly always based around these foods.

Because the Mediterranean Diet is high in fats and fruits, it is also high in the micronutrients of fatty acids and polyphenols, which studies have demonstrated can support healthy brain function.

So let's get real. Obviously eating an entire salmon and a bowl of berries isn't going to suddenly make you a genius overnight. However, choosing the foods listed in the Mediterranean Diet at least 80% of the time will go a long way to help you create a far healthier and better functioning body and brain. It won't take long before you are feeling so much better than when you eat those processed, sugar-laden, artificial creations labelled "food" that we find in the supermarket.

Not sure where to start? Rather than turning to a magazine to see what Khloé Kardashian is recommending this week, simply begin by adding protein to each meal. Unlike the other macronutrients (carbohydrates and fats), there are no large protein stores in the body so this nutrient needs to be consumed regularly. Protein is important as it contains the essential amino acids needed by the body to function including transporting vitamins and minerals around the body and balancing body fluids. A good protein intake helps you maintain your muscle mass, which also affects how your body uses food. It can help manage your appetite, as you feel more full when you eat steak compared to when you scoff a bowl of chips. Protein also supports your immune system and general wellbeing.

If you want to work out approximately how much protein you should include in your diet, the easiest way to find out the best plan for you personally is to book an appointment with a registered dietician. Otherwise, general guidelines for protein intake along with other nutrients can be found in the free, downloadable booklet "Nutrient Reference Values for Australia and New Zealand" available from the New Zealand Ministry of Health website.[12]

We affect our wellbeing and our ability to function at our best when our nutrition is not healthy, yet even though most of us understand this we still choose to eat crap.

Even more confusingly, we eat food when we are not actually hungry! We use it to distract ourselves or to procrastinate when we really should be getting stuck in and focused on what we are trying to achieve.

It's time to remove the complicated rules, the magazine diets and the negative emotions around food, and simplify how we eat so that we can get on with *rocking* our lives – healthy and happy!

ACTION TASKS:

- Protein first! At every meal, include a palm-sized portion of protein. There are so many choices! Meat, chicken, fish, eggs, tofu and more. Your body will thank you for it and you'll find that you feel more satisfied after every meal.
- Include more walnuts, berries and fatty fish like salmon in your diet. Studies have shown that the fatty acids found in the fish and the walnuts, along with the polyphenols found in berries, have been found to positively affect brain function.[13]
- Choose foods in their natural, unprocessed states. Artificial colors, sweeteners and chemical preservatives are bad for your health and should be avoided if you want to support your body and brain. Most of us enjoy a treat from time to time; however, if you can at least stick to the 80/20 principle of eating 80% healthy, whole food and 20% or less "treat" food, you will be setting yourself up for overall better health. Not sure where to start, and feeling overwhelmed by all of the diet plans out there? Consider meeting with a nutritionist to set up an eating plan personalized for you.
- Do you feel like food has become your procrastination outlet, or that you have lost control with your portion sizes? It is easy to find yourself raiding the fridge when you should be writing a challenging assignment. I talk from experience here as someone who works from home and has to stop herself from wandering to

the fridge whenever I get a bit stuck with my work! If you know that food has become an issue and you are eating for reasons other than to actually nourish your body and brain, be honest with yourself and decide to change your behavior. Some simple examples of changing your behavior might be: drinking sparkling mineral water instead of your regular soda fix; scheduling a walk or an exercise session at the time of day when you would normally head to the nearest fast-food outlet or bakery; changing your route to and from school or university if you are tempted by the hot donut shops on the way, and taking the time to chew your food a certain amount of times to break your habit of wolfing down huge portions mindlessly.

Removing both the behavior and the feelings of guilt and shame that go with it will free you up to truly focus on doing that thing you *want* to do with your life.

NOTE: If you know that your eating habits are controlling you rather than you controlling them, it's time to reach out for help. If you are finding yourself counting every calorie and exercising for hours, or bingeing uncontrollably and throwing up later, then speak to your parents, a trusted friend or your school counselor or nurse. There is no shame in admitting that food has become something that has a hold over you, and the quicker you can confront that hold and get back in control, the quicker you will start to create a life where you are happy and free of guilt and shame.

HACK #10

Drink that Water!

"Yeah, yeah," I hear you say. We all know that we should drink approximately eight cups a day, but do you actually do it?

And why the big deal?

Unfortunately, not many of us do drink enough water. Instead, we fill up with cups of coffee, juices or sodas, which are full of chemicals and sugar, and our bodies end up actually being dehydrated.

There have been lots of studies that show that dehydration of just 2% or more can make you feel tired, put you in a grumpy mood, and even affect brain functions like memory and the ability to concentrate.[14] These are not things you want your body to be dealing with when you are trying to focus on what you need to do to achieve your goal.

Right?

You generally lose around 4% of your body-weight in water every day, and the general suggestion of eight 250ml cups for women and ten for men helps meet this loss. Sculling too much water, however, can strip your minerals and electrolytes, which is why some folks recommend adding a pinch of Celtic sea salt to your water to replenish these important elements, instead of reaching for one of those advertised, bright-colored chemical cocktails called sports drinks. The condition of Hyponatremia, which refers to low blood sodium, is what we see occur in some high performance athletes who have competed in harsh, long marathons where their sodium levels are severely lowered through heat and dehydration. They are the ones you see staggering around like they are drunk before collapsing.

When you find yourself distracted and losing focus during the day, it's worth stopping and asking yourself if you are simply thirsty, rather than beating yourself up for not thinking straight. As well as this, how many times have you reached for a sugary snack or an energy drink when what you really needed was water because you were actually slightly dehydrated? A glass of water might be all you need to help you regain focus and get back on track with working towards your goal.

ACTION TASKS:

- Measure out a 250ml glass then keep a tally in your daily journal of how many of these you drink during the day. There's no need to be rigid and force yourself to drink – just use this exercise to make yourself aware of your water intake.
- Grab yourself a large glass or aluminum bottle before you leave home and measure how many of these you should be drinking. Again, keep a tally in your journal.
- Keep your bottle refilled and handy when you are out and about or in the classroom.
- Purchase some Celtic sea salt and add a half a teaspoon to each bottle or a pinch to each glass – you will barely taste the salt. And while you are at it, throw away any energy drinks or sports drinks that you might still have stashed in your fridge!
- Feeling thirsty? Drink up!
- Feeling tired, distracted or reaching without thinking for the cookie jar? Drink your water!
- Exercising hard and sweating? Increase your water intake and add a pinch of salt to each cup.

SECTION 4

TIME HACKS

"Time is the scarcest resource and unless it is managed nothing else can be managed."

~ PETER DRUCKER

"Time is at once the most valuable and the most perishable of all our possessions."

~ JOHN RANDOLPH

HACK #11

Prioritizing to reduce overwhelm!

If only I had a dollar for every time that I moaned that I didn't have "enough time" – especially when I had major essays due! Learning to "manage" time is probably one of the best things you can do while you are studying as it is a skill that will carry you through life, regardless of what career you head into.

There are heaps of "time management" systems out there, along with all of the arguments about which one is the best, which is the most simple to learn and which planner is the most efficient. As well, there is the debate about whether you should do all of your planning and scheduling online or in a paper diary. It's a bit like what we were talking about with nutrition plans, and makes me wonder how long it will be before a member of the Kardashian family starts selling diaries and planners!

The thing is though, regardless of whether you use

an online system or a paper diary to manage your social life and academic calendar – how many times have you started the year using your planner with great enthusiasm, only to give up around month four? Or are you one of those people who doesn't write anything down at all and attempts to keep all of your important dates in your head?

How's that working for you?

I think I'm pretty safe in guessing that it's not working too well at all.

Time management is a skill that helps us to get those things that we want to achieve done. Without understanding that time really *does* go by quickly, we allow ourselves to waste it and find ourselves at the end of each week wondering what on earth we actually achieved over those previous five days![15] This is certainly no way to *rock* your life!

Let's get real though: having a problem with "time management" is sugar-coating the fact that you really have a problem with "self management." Right? In fact, feeling like there is never enough time usually reflects a state that you might be in – the state of overwhelm.

Ever felt paralyzed by the sheer amount of work that you need to get done, so much so that you end up stuffing around looking "busy," like designing pretty title pages, but not actually doing the real work that your teacher set?

Or found yourself zoning out in front of Netflix when you know that you have three essays needing to be written?

Or even found yourself suddenly deciding to de-clutter

your wardrobe while the assignment that is due next week stays untouched?

These are all symptoms of a mind that is in a state of overwhelm, where the number of things that you need to do has gotten so huge that your "survival mode" brain now identifies them as being dangerous and harmful. Your brain is now trying to protect you by distracting you with easy, less stressful tasks like watching TV, snacking or gaming. If you don't learn to recognize what is happening, you will end up stuck: stuck not knowing how to break out of the rut you feel you that are in and stuck feeling like a fake who is not capable or worthy of achieving the dream you want to achieve.

Learning how to tackle the pile of work that is overwhelming you is the first step in taking control of your life. Once you have mastered the ability to identify, categorize, prioritize and schedule all of the tasks that you need to do you will find that your stress levels begin to drop because you will be able to get moving towards achieving your goal. You will feel calmer and more in control.

What is also exciting is that once you have mastered this process, you will be able to apply it in so many other areas of your life, whenever you feel overwhelmed by your workload. Whether you are in school or university, or at home, having the skills to organize and prioritize the huge list of things that you need to do will help make your ability to focus on what *really* matters way stronger. You won't be stuffing around getting nowhere anymore; instead, you will be *rocking* your life!

ACTION TASKS:

- A very easy way of managing the pile of assignments, study and chores that you are dreading is to find some time on your own and do a brain dump. In other words, write it all down! Just doing this simple task of dumping everything from your brain onto paper will make a huge difference to how you are feeling. You will be acknowledging all of the things that have been churning around in your brain, causing you to feel like crap.
- Use different colored pencils to shade or circle related items. For example, you might have a number of chores that you are expected to do every evening – ring these in green. You might have a number of training sessions and games for your chosen sport – circle these in blue. You get the idea.
- Now choose the most urgent task from each colored group and write them on a new page.
- Pull out your planner – paper or digital is fine (although I personally use both as the act of physically writing on paper helps my brain recall better). Choose a time for each of these most urgent tasks over the next week to be completed, but ONLY LIST ONE TASK A DAY.
- Keep these appointments with yourself exactly the same way that you would keep an appointment with your school principal. Once they are completed, tick them off – this is such a satisfying thing to do!

- At the end of the week, check which of the tasks were completed, reschedule those which need more time, and add one or two of the next level of urgent choices from your master list. This way you will be taking action on your main list and losing that feeling of being overwhelmed. You will also be breaking the habit of stuffing around that comes from the weight of having so many tasks to do.
- Celebrate at the end of the week when tasks can be completely removed from your master list!

HACK #12

Map Your Wheel of Life

> "The key is not to prioritize what's on your schedule, but to schedule your priorities."
>
> ~ STEPHEN COVEY

Have you ever sat down and thought about what your main priorities in life are, or do you find that you always feel like you are too busy trying to keep up with your assignments and chores to think about what you *really* want out of life?

Maybe you love photography, or rugby, or writing music – but you feel like you can never find the time to really get stuck into what *you* want to do as there always seems to be a stack of chores that your parents want you to do, or a ridiculously huge list of assignments and readings that your teachers want you to do.

Hopefully you have completed the huge brain dump of Hack #11, (if you haven't, head back there and do it now), and you've discovered that there are some important tasks that need to be done before you do anything else. However, while you know that you urgently need to complete an essay that is due tomorrow and study for a test the day after, you *really* want to go out and get some new soccer boots NOW!

So how do you work out where to begin and how to prioritize your time and energy?

Before I begin working with my life-coaching clients, I usually get them to complete what is called a "Wheel of Life" exercise. Originally created by a man called Zig Ziglar, the Wheel of Life shows us a picture of the key areas that most people have to deal with in their lives. The most common version of the wheel has eight different categories, although you can change these to suit your own situation. The idea is to ask yourself lots of questions about each category then give yourself a rating out of ten.

Once you have answered all of the questions and completed each category, you will have eight ratings. The lower ratings represent areas in your life that are more neglected, and the higher ratings show those areas that are going better. By sitting back and really looking at these ratings, you can see where your time and energy is focused and also what areas in your life need work.

For instance, you might rate yourself as going quite well in the areas of finance and recreation. Your part-time job is regular, you've been able to save a little each week and you are on track for buying that car next year that you have your eye on. As well as this, you've got a good group of mates and enjoy lots of gaming sessions with them, so your recreation category of life is great!

On the lower end of the scale, however, are the categories of romance and career/study. You broke up with your girlfriend a month ago and have been missing her, and you are struggling to stay focused at school plus feel totally clueless about what you want to do with your life.

Imagine a person who has been acting grouchy and feeling "blah" for a while seeing these findings about their life laid out clearly in a picture. Straight away they can see what areas of their lives need more time and effort, and they can start making decisions and taking action to make their lives better. They can now move on to goal setting and decision making, and choose where to best use their time.

Before you head into the action steps, grab a big piece of paper and draw a large circle. Draw lines to divide this circle into eight equal segments and then give these segments the following names:

1. Environment
2. Career/studies
3. Finances
4. Health and wellbeing
5. Relationships
6. Romance
7. Recreation
8. Personal development

As you work your way through the questions below, place a dot in the middle of each segment to show your rating. If the dot is near the center of the wheel, the rating is low. If the dot is near the circle edge, the rating is high. When finished, color in each segment to give a solid picture of the areas of your life that are rocking and those that could use some more attention and energy.

ACTION TASKS:

▶ Fill out your own Wheel of Life. Get creative and use different colors for each segment as you rate them. Here are the categories along with some questions that you can ask yourself:

Environment (where you live and where you work)**:** Are you in the middle of the city surrounded by noise and movement? Are you in the suburbs? Near the beach or in a rural setting? Is your physical environment at school or at home fun, depressing or neutral? How does your environment make you feel? Does it support to you to achieve the things that you want to achieve?

Career/studies: Are your studies helping you work towards a career that interests you or do you want to change direction? Do you know where you are going or are you totally feeling lost?

Finances: Are you earning enough to survive? Are you struggling? Do you want to earn more or are you happy with where you are at?

Health and wellbeing: How are you feeling physically? Are you eating and sleeping well? Do you drink enough water? Are you moving your body and exercising? Are you having regular wellness and dental check-ups?

Relationships: Do you make time to catch up with your family and your friends? Are there relationships that you have let slip and want to repair? Have you been so busy that you feel lonely? Do you feel like you don't have any close friends?

Romance: Are you wanting to find a girlfriend or boyfriend, but don't have the time? Are you unsure how to approach other people in a romantic way? Is your relationship with your current girlfriend or boyfriend strong, or have you been neglecting it?

Personal development: Are you the same person you were five years ago, or have you developed and matured in your thinking? Do you make time to read, learn and study things beyond what your teachers give you? Have you taken any new classes, be they academic, physical or artistic, to continue your personal development?

Recreation: Do you have regular social outings? Do you have any hobbies or pastimes that you enjoy? Do you allow time for these hobbies and fun activities in your schedule?

- Identify your three strongest areas and have a think about what is going well with them. Are they areas that can be maintained with less time? For example, you might have rated high in the area of recreation.

Maybe you could cut a bit of this time back to give more time for the areas that might be rating low such as your career/studies area?

- Identify your lowest three categories and write down just two things that you could do to improve the rating in these areas. For example, if you have rated low in personal development, two ways that you could improve in this area would be to listen to some motivating podcasts when you walk to school every morning, and subscribe to a YouTube channel that features a motivating speaker like Gary Vaynerchuk and commit to watching one of his videos each weekend.
- Take the ideas that stand out the most from each of the three lowest rated areas and list them on a separate page of paper.
- These items are now your most important priorities. They need your attention and energy so that you can improve the areas that are out of balance in your life. Now that you have identified them through this Wheel of Life exercise, you know exactly what you need to be focusing on. You can prioritize them in your timetable each week. You are now well on your way to creating a life that *rocks*!

HACK #13

Knock Off the Hard Stuff First!

Have you ever heard of "time-management teachers"? These folks teach you how to manage your time so that you can fit more in your day.

I've heard lots of them over the years, and they all have their own systems that work for them. The problem is though, what works for them doesn't necessarily work for you and me. They all seem to have their favorite "rules" too: "Don't listen to music before you've written your essay," "exercise first before you do anything else," "don't answer emails or check social media before noon," and so on.

Now don't get me wrong – all of these are good ideas, and I have personally tried each and every one of them at some stage. However, if you are anything like me, you probably find that trying to live perfectly simply sets you up for feeling like a failure, because who is able to live a perfect life?

For instance, let's say that I have decided to follow one time-management rule that dictates that I must no longer to check my social media or emails before noon. A message notification catches my eye, however, and without thinking, I answer it. How do I feel then? Pretty useless, and I start calling myself a failure. My day is ruined before it even begins.

It's exactly like when we decide that we are going to cut back on the crap food that we've been eating and start making healthy choices. We cave in and eat a small piece of chocolate cake that our grandma offers us, then beat ourselves up for being weak and go on to eat a ton of crap for the rest of the day.

When we give ourselves strict black-and-white rules to follow in any area of life, we generally set ourselves up to fail because it is very rare that life is ever completely black and white.

Let's now look at the reality of the "no social media and email before midday" rule. I personally run three online community groups, a large Facebook business page, and a few other social media sites where I connect and communicate with my audience. I'm also based in New Zealand, which means that a lot of action in these groups takes place during my sleeping hours. I find that I can't focus on my work for the day until I have checked what is happening in my groups.

What if there has been an argument in a group overnight that has caused members to leave? What if someone has decided to spam all the members? What if a member has reached out with a vulnerable message that needs an urgent reply? This particular rule just doesn't work for me.

On the other hand, we all know what a time suck that social media can be, don't we? So much time can be wasted scrolling and commenting, so instead I limit myself to an hour every morning to cover all of my groups, answering messages, checking member posts, and also checking my email accounts. In this hour, I delete any spam and highlight anything that I will need to respond to later in the day. Following this morning routine, social media channels are hidden and I am focused on my work.

As you can see, I applied the *principle* instead of a strict black-and-white rule that says there should be no social media before midday. My situation means that I do need to check my channels and mail before doing any work. However, I limit that time and stick to the *principle* of not letting social media distract me from the tasks that I need to do, by shutting it down immediately after I check in.

Life can be unpredictable can't it? It is very rare that two days are the same and if we tie ourselves up with too many strict rules, we set ourselves up to be failures – and who wants to live like that? Better to grab the principle or the idea behind a rule and apply that to your life to help you achieve better. For instance, if you can't exercise first thing in the morning, simply make sure that you exercise *somewhere* during your day, and I still suggest that you book it in your planner so that it is a daily priority. Personally speaking, if I am writing at home for an entire day I don't want to get in a car and lose a few hours going to the gym, so I do shorter bursts of exercise in between my work sessions at home. Being flexible in my thinking means that I don't beat myself up for not going to the gym, but I *do* stick to the principle of daily exercise by doing something at home.

Another time-management rule that always challenged me is the "tick the five hardest things off your list before 10 am" rule. I love this idea as I am one of the world's best at stuffing around and doing other activities instead of the "hard things" that I should be doing! However, trying to live by this hard and fast rule always backfires. It's exciting at first as I'm sure that this time, I am going to change my life. I then have a fantastic first few days where I proudly tick the five things off my list. However, something happens and I have to race the cat to the vet, or an appointment runs late, or my kid gets sick and I can't do what's on my list ... You get the idea. Very soon I no longer have five ticks in my planner every day, just a few ticks here and there.

And then I give up on it altogether, thinking I am a useless failure.

Again.

Instead, having learned the hard way that black-and-white rules don't work, I now use the *principle* of this rule to help me "get that hard thing done" every day. Whatever the number-one task is for the day, I aim to get it done first! This means that after I have done my morning check of all groups/channels/emails, I sit down and tackle the hardest task for the day. This is far easier to achieve than expecting to tick off five things every morning.

What's "hard" for you? For me, writing falls into this category. I actually love writing and time flies by once I am in the zone. Getting started, however, is a whole other issue. I will find myself scrolling Facebook, playing with graphics, cleaning my wardrobe out, inspecting my teeth in the mirror ... anything to avoid doing something that will require focus and effort.

Strange isn't it? If I set myself a strict black-and-white rule that says "no social media before writing and all writing has to be done before 11 am," I set myself up to fail. Instead, if I decide to "do the hard thing first" (after my morning routine of social media check in), I set myself up to win.

"But what if you have more than one 'hard thing?'" I hear you ask. This is where doing the brain dump exercise, followed by working out what your most important tasks are helps. I personally have a few "hard things" that are part of my business, so not only do I do them first, but I make each of them my main priority over different days of the week. This way, they all get the chance to be the "hard thing" that I tackle first. For you, it may mean identifying which of the assignments that are due soon is your "hard thing" that needs to be done first thing in your day.

ACTION TASKS:

- Out of the all of the tasks that you need to complete, list the ones that you consider to be "hard things."
- Write out the order of these tasks according to urgency. An assignment due this Friday will be more urgent than study for an exam next week. Then schedule them out over your week.
- Pat yourself on the back every time that you complete your "hard thing" first thing in the day. You will begin to feel more in control and successful each day that you can tick off your hard tasks.

HACK #14

Use a Timer!

Lots of time-management teachers suggest that one of the best ways to get your work done is in short spurts of activity. Working this way gives you a better chance of staying focused on what you are meant to be doing. You are less likely to be distracted and more likely to actually get stuff done.

One very popular method that teaches working like this is called the Pomodoro Technique. "Pomodoro" means tomato in Italian and the creator of this technique, a man called Francesco Cirillo, named his method after the tomato-shaped kitchen timer that he used. The Pomodoro Technique tells you to set a timer for 25 minutes, then work with 100% concentration until the timer rings. You then take a break and re-set your timer for the next 25 minutes.[16]

Now this all might sound a bit simple, but you'd be amazed at how working like this really does help people concentrate. Just thinking that you only have to focus for 25 minutes sounds a whole lot more doable than thinking that you have to write an essay that is going to take you hours, don't you think? As well as this, the more 25-minute blocks of work that you do the more successful you will feel, which will increase your confidence and self-belief.

Winning!

What's even better though is applying "the principle, not the rule" with this technique, just like we talked about in the last hack. You can take this concept of working in short, focused blocks of time and change the timings to suit you. I have personally come up with my own preferred method, which focusses on work-energy cycling. I combined my knowledge of personal training techniques with time-management methods like the Pomodoro Technique, to create what works for me, and you can use mine or create your own version too.

Let me explain. Are you someone who *really* struggles with staying focused on your work – especially if it is a subject that you don't enjoy? If so, I would suggest that you start out with shorter work-time blocks of 20 minutes where you shut down all distractions and focus hard. You could then follow this 20-minute block with a longer interval of less intense activity that is still directly related to the project you are working on. You would then cycle these high and low intensity sessions until you have completed whatever your assignment is for the day. I think of this being like HIIT (high intensity interval training) exercise programs, where people who are working out alternate short bursts of hard physical exercise that raises their heart rates with less intense sessions where their heart rates slow down again.

An example of working like this might be that you write your essay for 20 minutes straight. You then follow this with 30 minutes of reading and research about the topic that you are writing on. You might then take a 5-minute break to refill your drink bottle and have a stretch before starting your next 20-minute, high energy writing block.

Get the idea?

Perhaps you find that you need longer to really get stuck into your work? You might decide on trying 40-minute focused blocks with a 10-minute break afterward, before beginning a following 50–60-minute block. The first 40 minutes would require higher energy input, the following 50–60, lower. The great thing is that you can change the times to best suit how *you* like to work. You just adjust the lengths of the three blocks: high energy/focus, low energy/focus and a break.

Find yourself a unique song or alarm tone that you can use to keep you on track with your time – especially your breaks, as you don't want these to blow out! Soon you will find that this self-applied HIIW – *high intensity interval working* – technique becomes an automatic way of working for you. You will also find that you are steadily knocking off those chores and assignments and moving towards reaching your goal of getting passing grades that will allow you to create your life that *rocks*.

However, be warned – setting a timer is still not going to stop the number-one source of interruptions and distractions to you getting your work done: your brain. While you can put your phone on silent and switch off all social media notifications so they don't distract you and break your focus, it is much harder to turn your brain off. I don't know about you, but I am constantly wrestling to keep my thoughts focused on the task that I am meant to be working on. Even while writing this paragraph I have caught myself wondering what appointments I have this week, thinking about the calls I need to make tomorrow, debating what I am going to cook for dinner tonight and pondering what a fabulous life my cats have as I watch them snooze on the floor by my feet as I sit at my desk.

This battle with our brains is similar to another battle lots of us have experienced. Ever decided to stop eating chocolate and all of a sudden found that it is all that you can think about? If we label our thoughts as "enemies" that we need to fight and overcome to stay focused on our work, we will always be in a no-win situation where we constantly beat ourselves up and feel like failures. Certainly no way to *rock* your life! Instead, try appreciating the fact that your brain is creative and clever, and rather than wasting energy trying to fight your thoughts away, have a piece of paper next to your work station where you can write them down immediately. That way you can get straight back into your work, knowing that you will come back to those thoughts in your break.

Finding your own unique HIIW method will not only

help you stop stuffing around and get *doing* that thing you should be doing, it will also bring a huge feeling of achievement and satisfaction as you get more and more of your work completed. And it all begins with getting yourself a timer!

ACTION TASKS:

- Find a unique sound to use for your timer bell on your phone, raid the kitchen supplies or purchase a fun kitchen timer.
- Have a notepad and pen on your desk next to your timer to write down the random thoughts that will try to distract you. Jot them down quickly then get straight back to what you are working on. You can give them more thought in your break.
- Choose your main focus each day, and create a list of the high energy tasks and low energy tasks associated with this focus. For example, your focus might be a history essay, and the tasks you need to do might include reading and research, interviewing people, drafting, then writing the essay and compiling a bibliography. You would then divide these tasks into high and low intensity.
- Choose the length of your high and low energy time blocks, set your timer and begin! Just starting out or find that you struggle to keep your mind on your task? Choose shorter lengths of time for your high focus session, and then congratulate yourself every time that you complete one.
- At the conclusion of each work block, use your break time to check through the list of the random thoughts that you wrote down on your note pad. What needs to be sorted right away and what needs to be added to your planner for later?
- Grab some water, have a stretch, reset that timer and get going again!

SECTION 5

ATTITUDE HACKS

"Ability is what you're capable of doing.
Motivation determines what you do.
Attitude determines how well you do it."

~ LOU HOLTZ

HACK #15
Find Your Cape

There have been many researchers who have set out to discover the links between people's personalities and their behavior of stuffing around or procrastinating. One study even estimated that the percentage of university students who struggle with procrastination is as high as 70–95%![17]

Procrastination, or stuffing around doing anything and everything *except* what you should be doing, affects just about everyone. Even the person with the most exciting dream of creating a life that totally *rocks* is not immune to it. It seems crazy that we procrastinate even when we are working on tasks that will help us achieve what we really want – like graduating – but so many of us still do.

We've already looked at some practical hacks to help break this negative habit, but there is another area of our life that really affects procrastination. If we don't stop and understand this area, regardless of what clever time management principles we use, we will always find ourselves stuffing around instead.

The area we need to look at? It is the area of our own self-belief.

If you believe deep down that you are not worthy of doing well you will subconsciously stuff up your progress, and procrastination is one of the most effective ways of doing this. For instance, even though you might say that you want to graduate well from school so that you can get into university, or graduate with a first-class degree so that you can get a great job, you might subconsciously feel that you don't actually deserve this. Chances are, if you don't address this inner belief then you will act in a way that that confirms this belief and you really *won't* succeed.

Maybe you hold a secret inner belief that achieving your goal could make others in your friend or family circles feel less about themselves. The old saying that "you don't need to dim your light for others to shine brightly" exists because of this very belief. Girls especially can find themselves holding themselves back without realizing that they are doing it. They might not know the reason why, but a bit of digging might reveal that they don't want to shine too brightly in case they draw the spotlight away from their boyfriend, their best friend or their classmates.

It seems silly to read in black and white, yet I know so many people who subconsciously think like this. It's a bit like the "tall poppy syndrome" that affects Kiwi and

Aussie cultures on so many levels. This syndrome means that people get nervous about being the "tall poppy" that stands higher than all of the others, as that is the one that gets its head lopped off. In real life, this might hold you back from being a high achiever in case others notice and start to say you are full of yourself!

There is another inner belief that can affect your "self-efficacy." Having a strong, positive self-efficacy means that you have the belief that you *can* actually achieve the goal that is in front of you. Researchers have discovered that a person's self-efficacy can directly affect their ability to perform well in any area in life.[18]

If, deep down, you truly don't *believe* that you are capable of completing a task, you will fail to take control of your time and energy. Instead, you will subconsciously stuff up your efforts to do the work that you *should* be doing to create the life that you want, and procrastinating is one of the main ways to do this.

To fight this, I'm declaring that it is time to find yourself a cape – just like the ones that every superhero wears.

Not literally, of course – although if you still have one tucked at the back of your wardrobe from when you were a kid, pull it out!

I can guarantee that you believe in some other people, believing that they are smarter, more talented, more worthy and more capable than you. I'm here to remind you though that they are still just people. It's time for you to believe in yourself too!

It's time to kick those inner lies to the curb. You ARE

worthy of success, and even if you don't yet have the skills, you ARE capable of learning them along with whatever is needed in order to do that thing you are wanting to do to *rock* your life!

ACTION TASKS:

▶ Retrain your brain! Go back to the very first hack of this book, the one about visualization, and use this technique to create a mental picture of yourself. This time however, I want you to really focus on seeing yourself *doing* those steps and tasks that you need to master to achieve your goal. This is the same technique that athletes use when they are trying to master a new skill.

As an example, my daughter represented New Zealand numerous times as a junior aerobic gymnast and she would practice visualization, not only before a competition where she would run her full routine mentally numerous times, but also as part of the process of learning any new skills. Being able to picture herself completing the skill and "feeling" how the skill was meant to be executed meant that when it came time to attempt the skill physically, her body responded quickly, already knowing the pathway it needed to follow. Importantly though, her visualization also strengthened her "self-efficacy" – her belief that she *was* capable of mastering this task. Likewise, when I was learning difficult passages of music for exams I would picture the notes and feel the patterns in my fingers while sitting on public transport for hours at a time to get to and from the Conservatorium. My self-efficacy – or self-belief that I would master this piece and play it perfectly on stage – increased every time that I pictured myself performing it.

- Decide to start speaking well to and about yourself. Whenever you feel yourself starting to stuff around and procrastinate, check your thinking. Are you believing deep down that you are not worthy of or good enough to achieve what you are aiming for? If so, step away and apply the breathing technique from Hack #3, then tell yourself out loud that you *are* capable of doing the task that you need to do.
- You've completed the above steps? Time to show a bit of tough love to yourself now. Sit your butt down and DO the thing you are meant to be doing! It might feel like you are wading through thick, sludgy mud as you get going, but if you can keep reminding yourself that you *are* capable, you *are* worthy and you definitely are *not* giving up, you will find that your attitude and your procrastination habit will change. You will begin to enter a state where the sludgy-mud sensation melts away as your creative juices begin to flow.

It's time to rock your cape so you can *rock* your life!

HACK #16
Establish Your Boundaries

Have you ever heard of "people pleasers?"

Maybe you are one? Not sure? Then ask yourself this question: "Are you so busy trying to do what *others* want you to do that you don't seem to have the time or ability to focus on completing the thing *you* want to achieve?"

If this is you, you are definitely not alone! Many people, girls especially, but many boys too, fall into this trap. They find that they give so much of their time and headspace to other people's needs that they not only struggle to achieve that thing they are *really* wanting to do, but they develop feelings of angry resentment towards others *and* towards themselves.

Having boundaries is your best defense against being a people pleaser. A physical boundary like a fence around a house prevents unwelcome visitors and a boundary around your time does the same. It means that you are protecting the time that you have committed to what you should be doing. Your boundary protects this time, regardless of if your bestie suddenly wants to come over and moan about their latest boyfriend/girlfriend problems.

Admittedly, starting to use boundaries can feel selfish when you are used to putting other people's needs before your own. Even more so when the thing you want to do is new and special because it is something that you have never before achieved. It can feel strange saying "no" to a friend who wants you to come and hang out, because it is the only time that you have to write and you've never actually written a book before. It can feel wrong to let others down over something you don't even know that you are capable of doing!

The thing is though, if you truly want to achieve that goal and *rock* your life, you need to put in place the boundaries required to give you the space you need to make your dream happen.

One of the presentations that I deliver as a professional speaker is called "Are you living your life in 3D?" In this presentation I talk about the "voices" in your world that have the ability to affect you and the choices you make for your life. One of these outside "voices" is the "Voice of Distraction." This is the voice that tells you that you should be doing everything and anything *other* than that thing that you know deep down that you *should* be doing. Having boundaries that help you resist this voice is so important, as often this particular voice will come from a well-meaning friend or family member who thinks that they are helping by suggesting that you follow their idea. It's these people who are the hardest to say "no" to.

It's well known that a plane that flies just one degree off course will end up in an entirely different location to the one that it was meant to be heading for. Listening to a "Voice of Distraction" can set you off your course and, before you know it, you will find yourself nowhere near achieving the thing that you had wanted to achieve. Instead, you will be busy fulfilling someone else's agenda. As the saying goes, if you don't follow your own dreams, someone else will get you to follow theirs.

Let's say that your dream is to go to art school and become a professional painter. Your "Voice of Distraction" could be your well-meaning dad who suggests that you take up an apprenticeship with his mate who is looking for someone to work in his automotive business. Or it could be your best friend who is pushing you to go to the same university with them instead – one that doesn't have the subjects that you want.

The way to prevent a "Voice of Distraction" from sending you off target is to have firm boundaries in place. Boundaries that will help you stay on course. Boundaries that will help you protect the time, headspace and focus you need in order to do the work YOU want and need to do.

Setting such boundaries can feel selfish, but they are you showing yourself self-care. You are showing yourself and others that you value your time, your feelings and your purpose. You are demonstrating to the world that YOU determine the agenda for your own life, not somebody else.

Healthy boundaries – and NOT rigid, inflexible, unhealthy ones that mean you don't listen to anyone else's input and wisdom – are essential if you are going to develop and maintain the laser focus you need to work and reach your goal.

Healthy boundaries mean that you value your own goals and are able to stand by your own decisions. They also mean that you won't be swayed from your values or get caught up in other people's agendas, no matter how well-meaning they might sound.

ESTABLISH YOUR BOUNDARIES 99

ACTION TASKS:

- What are the "set-in-concrete" priorities in your life? Time with your girlfriend or boyfriend? Time to train for your sport? Time to work at your personal goal – that thing that you want to achieve? Write them down on a list, along with some ideas of what these set-in-concrete priorities look like in an average week. Some examples might be: an hour of chill-out time whenever you get home from school, before you start your assignments; an outing or a date once a week with your girlfriend or boyfriend; a sports game every weekend; or an hour every second day to work on your book/your painting/your body at the gym.
- Schedule times for all of these priorities over the next month. I still use a paper journal as well as an online calendar and find that I am even clearer on how my week is looking when I use different colors for each type of time block.
- Stand your ground and protect these time blocks! Sometimes there will be a valid reason for things changing, but this next month is the time for you to begin to flex those self-care, boundary-enforcing muscles.
- Once you have identified these time-focused boundaries, begin to look at other areas of your life. Where else have you let your boundaries be trampled over? Is it in the classroom, in group projects where you always seem to be the only one doing all the

work? Is it in friendships where you feel like you are always dragged into other people's dramas?
- Make a list of the areas in your life where you know that you need to put some boundaries in place, and decide today that you are going to start holding them firm – even if it it just one boundary at a time.

HACK #17

Choose Your Mood

There are many tools and methods that people use to identify and understand different personalities. When we understand our own personality and how other people are different from us, we find it easier to communicate with them.

One personality-profiling tool is the Myers-Briggs method. It looks at the different way that people think and feel and make decisions. Two of the different personality types that this method talks about are "thinkers" or "feelers." A thinking person tends to be more rational about how they make decisions and a feeling person makes decisions based on how they feel.[19] Neither is better than the other – they are simply different.

I'm a mom to two adults now, but when they were younger they showed very different personalities. One child presented more strongly as a feeler while the other was a thinker and more similar to my husband and myself. As we mature though, our personalities become more balanced and most people have different degrees of both thinking and feeling traits.

Regardless of whether you are a thinker or a feeler you are going to face challenges when it comes to getting stuck into the work that you need to do, *especially* when it requires lots of focus. You certainly don't need to do a personality test to know that doing your calculus homework is a task that you would be happy to skip!

However, for feelers in particular, the mood that you are in at any moment can stop you from getting stuck into what you *should* be doing. When you are "not in the mood," or are instead bored, tired, grumpy or *whatever*, you run the chance of messing up your life by choosing to give into your feelings. It is so important to realize that feelings play a strong part in shaping your decision making and they can hold you back from doing what is important *if you let them.*

If you let your moods control when you will and won't work, you will never complete a project. Besides, if you are really honest, regardless of whether you are a thinker or feeler, you go through multiple moods and feelings each day – right?

- Feeling hungry?
- Itchy?
- Uncomfortable?
- Bored?
- Ticked off at your parents?
- Stressed at your teacher piling on the assignments?

- Jealous of your friend who got chosen for the sports team that you missed out on?

If you allow these moods the chance, they will become excuses that prevent you from taking action, and there is no way that you will be able to create a life that *rocks* if you don't take action.

"I'm not in the mood."

These five words can stop productive behavior dead in its tracks. Say it with a whiney, child-like tone (Go on, I dare you!), and you will realize what you are *really* dealing with: your inner spoiled brat.

Every one of us has been a brat at some stage – if you think this doesn't apply to you, just ask your parents! However, most of us learn to control our inner brat as we grow up so that we can play nicely with others. Unfortunately though, that control slips when we are trying to do tasks that require hard work, and that's when our bratty self who runs on feelings kicks in. We end up stuffing ourselves up by using our favorite procrastination techniques.

Game session instead of essay writing, anyone?

Texting instead of maths homework?

Have you ever seen a young child behave themselves for their teacher then throw a tantrum as soon as they get home to their parents? We sometimes unconsciously follow this same pattern of behavior – yes, really! We focus hard for our teachers, and then we throw an inner tantrum and can't be bothered when it is time to work hard for ourselves out of school hours.

If we don't learn to control how we react to our moods and feelings, we will never be able to get going and create the rocking life that we want. We will find ourselves stuck in a cycle of procrastination, feeling like crap and beating ourselves up when everyone else seems to be getting ahead in life.

ACTION TASKS:

- Try to catch yourself stuffing around when you should be working on a task that requires focus.
- Stop and ask yourself, "What am I feeling?" If those feelings are negative, stop and have a think about *why* you are feeling that way. Are they irrational, are you just having a bit of a tantrum, or is there a valid reason for feeling that way? (I need to add too that if you are feeling dark, negative thoughts all the time for no rational reason, this is heading into a whole different area – that of mental health. Your first step here should be to reach out to a trusted health professional for advice.)
- If there is something that you need to face, like an unresolved argument, for example, write it down. Doing this means that you are acknowledging the feeling and promising yourself that you will deal with the situation later on.
- If it is hunger or thirst, sit back and ask yourself whether these are true feelings or if you are simply stuffing around. If they are true feelings, set your timer to complete your work block and promise yourself that you will stop and enjoy a fantastic lunch once you have completed that session of focused work.
- If there is no real reason why you are feeling "blah," change your physical state. Get out of your chair, do some star jumps and push-ups. Get that heart pumping and you will find that your mood gets a whole lot better!

- Decide that you are no longer going to give into your inner brat who doesn't *feel* like working! It's time they were taught who is boss, so tell your inner brat to be quiet and sit in the corner when they are screaming at you that they don't *feel* like working!

SECTION 6

ACCELERATION HACKS

"Start by doing what's necessary;
then do what's possible; and suddenly
you are doing the impossible."

~ FRANCIS OF ASSISI

HACK #18
Create Systems

As a student, one of the best things that you for yourself is create systems around the tasks you do frequently. Like the process of de-cluttering that we talked about in Hack #4, creating systems can take a bit of time to do; however, once set up, they will streamline your life. In fact, I have learned the hard way how *not* taking the time to create and use systems to manage the tasks in your life is only going to bite you on the butt down the track.

Not creating systems means that you will find yourself going over and over the same activities, wasting time and wasting creative energy that could have been applied to actually *doing* the thing you are really wanting to do. Want to be a writer? Why waste your time trawling the net to find the same writing groups each time, when you should be actually *writing?!*

Be honest now, how many times have you played guess-the-password for various websites or wasted time retyping all of the same hashtags for a social media post?

Systems and processes help you to free up so much of your time, meaning that you can get on with the creative work that you should be doing instead of wasting time. Unfortunately though, we put off taking the time to create these systems, as we are "too busy" chasing our tails and doing all of the last-minute things instead.

Feeling too overwhelmed by how much work you need to complete to graduate this year and don't know where to start?

My best advice – learned from the hard experience of trying to do everything myself – is to hire a tutor or enroll in a weekly online course that helps you tackle the work you need to do to graduate. Sure, there is plenty of free information available; however, at some point, you need to ask yourself if spending hours online trying to teach yourself how to write the perfect essay is *really* the best use of your time! Even if you are not too bad at a certain subject, getting a few hours of expert input on how to research, structure an essay or understand algebraic formulas will make a world of difference. Investing in a few tutoring sessions with a specialist to help you learn how to systematically research, construct and edit a top-grade essay could save you months of stuffing around on your own!

There are as many ways of streamlining your life as there are individuals, but I have put together a check list of ideas to get you thinking. Chances are, you will read some suggestions like "make your bed" and wonder what on earth that has to do with systems and processes to help you achieve your goal. Trust me though, each suggestion listed has the ability to decrease the amount of clutter that you face every day, be it physical, mental or even in cyberspace. As we have already discussed, clutter creates sensory overload and overwhelm. Sorting and removing much of this clutter is one thing, but putting in place new systems to maintain and manage your life going forward will help take away many of the distractions that are stopping you from focusing on actually *doing* what you are meant to be doing.

Personal Systems Tips

Put your clothes out the night before. If you're wanting to make a real difference, save time and effort by keeping a reduced selection of clothes.

If you are going to a gym before any classes or lectures, have those bags packed and ready the night before. Make sure that you don't forget any of the basics – phone chargers, sunglasses, reading glasses, wallets, inhalers, mints, hair brushes and personal items – or any planners and work due to be turned in.

Have your car keys or bus card and a water bottle ready to be grabbed on your way out.

Keep a notebook on you at all times. Jot down any dates, appointments and ideas, and then add them to your main planner every evening.

Review your planner every night and keep a master list in it of all of the things that cross your mind that you need to do. Every subject, assignment and chore – dump them into this list.

If you cook for yourself, start the habit of cooking enough food for your evening meal so that you can pack your lunch with the leftovers at the same time, ready for the next day. If you eat with your family, talk to your parents about having enough food for your lunches.

Have a regular day scheduled in your planner once a fort- night or once a month, depending on your needs, when you book your personal appointments like doctors, dentists and hairdressers.

Keep all incoming notices in the same location on your desk and sort (and throw out as necessary) notices as soon as they come in the door. In the same way, keep track of all receipts or notices in your email inbox as soon as they come in so that you can locate them all when you are ready to pay them attention.

Give yourself 10–15 minutes every night to clear the kitchen surfaces, bathroom surfaces and your study desk or work area of an evening before you head to bed.

Always make your bed of a morning.

Wipe down your bathroom surfaces with your used towel after showering before throwing it in the washing pile.

At least twice a year, thoroughly sort your medications, makeup, skin products and bathroom cabinet contents (I usually do this during spring and autumn).

Office Systems Tips

Tidy your desk whenever you have finished working. This goes for both at home and at school or uni.

Keep a drink bottle and coaster at your desk, along with a packet of mints.

Make sure that you have any stationery like spare pens, refill paper, holes punches, sticky tape, pencils, sharpeners and erasers at your desk.

If you use in-trays to collect assignments and notes, create a regular time each day to sort these and use the "one-touch" method, which means that once you pick that piece of paper up, you delegate, work on or dispose of it immediately.

Online Mail Tips

Every time that a newsletter lands in your inbox that you don't want to or don't have the time to read, unsubscribe immediately.

Create folders to move any receipts or membership information into immediately after payment.

Create folders for different categories of emails that need to be saved for future reference, e.g. domain information, passwords, school library links, online courses and product information.

Decide what time of day you are going to check your email and stick to those times. Personally, I like to check in the morning, again around noon then again in the late afternoon.

Turn off email notifications on your devices.

Social Media Tips

Batch the creation of professional-looking Instagram posts using apps like Canva and Wordswag if you are wanting to build a following. You can create great images and title pages for your assignments in these apps too.

Restrict checking social media sites to certain times of day. Again, I tend to do this morning, noon and evening.

When you are checking social media at your allocated times, instead of scrolling aimlessly, work your way systematically through your groups and key pages, replying to comments and private messages immediately.

If you are someone who is easily distracted by social media, establish the rule of not consuming before you create. In other words, do the work that requires most of your attention and focus *before* you scroll through other people's lives, views and opinions.

Business Tips

If you are a business owner – even if just a newspaper run – understand that systems are the backbone to any successful business and learn to treat even your smallest part-time venture with respect. You will learn so much from managing your small business that you will be able to transfer into the working world when you have graduated.

Keep track of your weekly income and expenses.

Ensure that you save a portion of your income *before* you pay for any expenses or make purchases. Some financial experts suggest saving at least 10% of your income.

ACTION TASKS:

- Go through the checklists above. Are there any tasks that you do regularly that really jump out as being hotspots in your world that need to have systems put in place? They might be systems to help you with filing and storing knowledge, or systems that help you stay on top of the clutter in your room.
- Highlight these tasks and brainstorm some ideas about how you could apply systems to them. Do this on paper so that you are actively engaged in the process.
- Choose three of these hotspots and work out how to set up systems to make them flow more efficiently over the next week. An example might be figuring out how you deal with all of the notes that come home from school:
  a) Every afternoon, check your bag and all of your pockets for notes and place them in one tray.
  b) Using the "one-touch" method, check each note and decide if it needs a response, needs to be delegated to a parent, or has a date for you to add to your planner before throwing it out.
  c) Place notes that you need to respond to back in the tray and notes delegated to your parents in another tray.
- At the end of that first week, review your new systems and tweak them it they need to suit you better. Then identify another two or three hotspots that you need

to tackle and draft on paper, systems that you could create to make those hotspots in your life work better.
- Reach out to someone who is great at applying systems. They might be a parent, an uncle or aunt, a friend or a teacher who can assist you to set up systems that help you stay up to date with getting those regular things that you need to do done efficiently and effectively.

HACK #19

Create Your Dream Team

Setting out to chase your dream and create a life that *rocks* can be a lonely journey. Chances are you won't be texting all of your friends to let them know that you are going to become a professional athlete, write your first book, create your first art exhibition or build your first business until you've reached a stage in the process where you know that you *will* do it. (Unless, of course, you are one of those social media come-with-me-for-the-ride influencers – in which case, be prepared for the public pressure comes along with that role!) Even your teachers, family and closest friends will possibly think you are either nuts or full of BS.

We all know that when you chase a dream there is that very real chance of failing. Failing is the risk that *everyone* who wants to achieve something faces. The more public the fail, however, the more embarrassing, and when you've failed a few times it gets harder to motivate yourself to try again. This is a big reason why many of us tend to keep our dreams and goals to ourselves. We find time around our other work and chores to work towards our goals privately, but the problem with doing this on your own is that with no one to push or challenge you it becomes very easy to get lazy or give up altogether.

As a private person who really doesn't like telling the world my personal goals, I *totally* understand why people want to keep things close. Whenever I go to start writing a new book or try a new sport or hobby, the last place that I go to is social media to tell the world! The problem, however, is that the path to creating an extraordinary life where you are chasing your dreams is already a lonely one.

Look around you. How many of your friends are trying to create something special with their lives and how many are just coasting along, taking what comes? I would suspect that the number in the last group is larger than that in the first group, which is where you fit.

Right?

The very fact that you are reading this book tells me that you are one of the few who really want something different out of life. Unfortunately though, it is easy to get a bit lost when you are too much in your own world. Moving forward is so much harder when you are stuck in your own head, which is why it is so critical to create a dream team – your very own group of trusted people who can bring insight and wisdom to your life.

A dream team may have a friend or two in it, but really, the key people you want in your dream team are people that you *respect*. They are people who will not only encourage you, but will also challenge you to do better. They may be people your age, or not. They may be family and friends, or not.

Let me give you an example by describing my own dream team. My team consists of my husband, my business mentors, my publisher, three close friends who are also entrepreneurs and speakers, and two trusted assistants who help me with the technical side of things.

Then there is the next layer of key people that I trust: my doctor who I've known for over 20 years, my lawyer and accountant as well as some key friends here in New Zealand and overseas who I know I can reach out to any time.

If you are really going to stop stuffing around and create a life that *rocks*, you need to start asking yourself these questions:

> "Who are the people I *want* and who are the people that I *need* in my dream team?"

> "Who are the people who I can trust, confide in, ask advice from and moan to when the going gets hard?"

> "Who will hold me accountable when I am stuffing around and not getting the work done to actually achieve my goal?"

For instance, let's say that your goal is to build a strong athletic body. Having worked in the fitness industry for years, I have seen many people with this desire and, in general, those who built a dream team around them had the best rate of success. As a personal trainer, I heard many of the hopes, dreams, health history, and emotional ups and downs of those clients who included me as part of their dream team. My job was to encourage, instruct, motivate, sometimes plead with them not to give up, and at other times provide a kick up the butt! All this as well as my main job, which was to design their exercise programs and keep track of their progress.

A person with the goal of building a strong, athletic body might create a dream team that consists of:
- A nutritionist
- A personal trainer
- A mentor or friend who has achieved this same goal.
- A supportive partner and/or close friend
- A GP or health professional
- A workout buddy

What is the goal that you are wanting to achieve? Try to look at it with new eyes and work out the steps you need to get there – the same way that an architect creates a design, but then the builder works out the actual program to bring the design to reality. In the same way that a roof can't go on if there are no footings and frames, what is the order of the steps that you need to go through to achieve your goal?

Next, what knowledge and expert input do you need to help you build those steps?

Finally, do you know and trust these experts already or will you need to find them?

Understand that creating your dream team is different to simply using professionals to fulfil certain tasks. I will be using a designer and a printer for this book at some stage, but they are not part of my dream team. Those roles are reserved for people who I trust and have a relationship with, and who I know have my best interests at heart.

The people I want on my dream team also have wisdom and credibility from achieving in their own areas of expertise.

Here are some suggestions for dream team members:
- A family member
- Your closest friend
- Your closest medical professional
- Your trainer
- Your nutritionist
- Your lawyer
- Your financial advisor or accountant
- Your business mentor or coach
- Your art teacher
- Your writing coach
- Your music or theatre producer
- Your agent or manager
- Your contemporary in another city or country
- You most inspiring teacher or lecturer

ACTION TASKS:

- Write out your goal and the steps that you need to take to achieve it. What kinds of people do you think you will need to add to your dream team?
- Write a list of the people you already know who would fit each of the steps that you have to cover.
- Make contact with each person on your list and talk to them about their importance in your life. Buy them lunch, share the story of the goal that you are wanting to achieve and listen to whatever wisdom they have to share.
- If there are people that you feel should be on your team but you don't know who they are, go through your networks and find the people who you think would fit. Do any of your friends know this person and could introduce you? It may take time, but these new people can be part of your outer layer while you build a relationship with them.

SECTION 7

ACTION HACKS

"There are risks and cost to action. But they are far less than the long-range risks of comfortable inaction."

~ JOHN F. KENNEDY

HACK #20
Intentional Action

Let's say that the thing that you are wanting to do is to write a book.

You follow your favorite authors on Amazon, stalk their websites and get onto their mailing lists.

You follow popular writing blogs and leave lots of well-thought responses.

You follow even more writers on Facebook and Instagram, and engage in literary discussions.

You join author-support groups online and encourage one another as you all talk about *why* you want to write your books, *who* your books are aimed at and *which* writing software is best to use.

You have a backlog of uncompleted "How to Write" courses.

You are an active member in online groups debating self-publishing over traditional publishing, along with every possibility in between.

You've spent hours cruising book-cover designs and have drawn multiple designs of your own.

You've listened to dozens of podcasts and know all about the best methods of marketing and promoting your book.

You are doing everything except WRITING the darn thing!
You see what's happening here? You are taking plenty of action, but if your goal is to complete a book, none of this action is actually moving you towards achieving this goal! (Hey, I'm speaking from experience here – don't judge!)

Let's try another scenario. Remember that strong, athletic body that we talked about? Let's say that you want to build one of those so you can really *rock* at your sport.

You might know the details of every gym within a 10 mile radius of your home.

You may understand all about the multiple diets that are featured in every magazine at the moment.

You might have researched every exercise plan available.

You may have the best gym wear, shoes and various bits of equipment floating around your house.

HOWEVER, you have never actually committed to DOING the work every day that is needed to transform and strengthen your body.

See the pattern here?

It is so easy to fill every minute of time that we have with "busy" work that seems related to the goal that we are wanting to complete, but that isn't actually getting the real work done. If we aren't completely honest with ourselves, and also aren't open to having a member of our dream team tell us the truth, we can end up months or even years down the track, no closer to actually achieving our goal and certainly nowhere near having a life that *rocks*!

Instead, we'll find ourselves frustrated and confused, wondering why all of the hours that we have spent supposedly working on our goal have come to nothing.

Have you heard the expression "work ON your business, not IN your business?" This refers to the problem of business owners getting so caught up in the day-to-day, minor activities of their business that someone else could easily do, that they lose sight of the bigger picture and their business suffers as a result. All this while they are crying that they are too busy to scratch themselves.

The principle is the same when it comes to you achieving that goal that *you* want to achieve. If you get so caught up researching, reading and spending hours on tasks that are not *directly* related to the goal you are aiming for, you will be actively holding your progress back. Time is so precious – trust me on this one, or ask anyone over the age of 40! You only have a limited amount of it to use towards bringing your dreams to reality. Being busy, but not in a way that is moving you towards actually achieving your goal, is a negative habit to fall into, and the quicker you can break it, the quicker you will start making progress.

Remember how we talked about the trap of trying to do everything yourself, especially when you are just starting out on your goal? If your entire time is spent learning and working on various tasks that are not 100% in line with directly working towards your goal, you will never see that goal achieved. Sure, you might have an impressive website, lots of fans on your amazing social media, an active support group of people all working towards a similar goal and even a perfectly immaculate bedroom, but if your dream was to write a book, build a business, hold your own art exhibition or invent a device that helps save the environment, NONE of these other things will have helped in the least. They are all non-urgent tasks that are best outsourced to others, or, at the very least, worked on AFTER you have completed your main objective.

The saying that "any action is better than no action" doesn't really fly these days. You might feel that doing *something* is better than doing nothing at all; HOWEVER, as we have already discussed, action for the sake of action will only keep you busy, and will not help you get any closer to where you ultimately want to be. You will have wasted time, money and energy, all of which are usually in short supply in your teen years.

Better to rework that saying to "any *intentional action* is better than no action at all." Even if the action you take isn't perfect, if it is specific, targeted and focused on the goal you are aiming for, it is still going to have far more impact than if you had not done anything at all. This way, if you are having a tough day where time is short and your brain isn't really engaged, you can manage to get some work done towards the fulfilment of your dream goal. It might not be a "perfect" day, but the action you take is still moving you towards your goal.

ACTION STEPS:

- What is the one MAIN task that you should be doing to work towards your goal?
    Writing?
    Painting?
    Creating a business plan?
    Composing music?
    Writing your assignments?
    Memorizing that new language?
    Lifting those weights?
    Practicing that instrument?
  If you are unsure, meet with one or more members of your dream team who have achieved a similar goal to what you want to achieve and work it out with them.

- Write your main task down on a large piece of paper in the form of a question. For example, "Have you written/practiced/worked out/studied/painted today?" Make it bright, creative and eye-catching, then stick it on the side of your bathroom mirror, in your kitchen, in your school locker or wherever you are guaranteed to see it every day.

- Commit yourself to focused chunks of time where you will actually DO your intentional action, although I suggest you underestimate your output at first. You may commit to just completing one 20-minute session a day at first; however, during that block of time you will be working ONLY on the key task that you need to complete to achieve your goal. You will be amazed at how far five straight days of working like this will propel you in comparison to the hours of distracted, unfocused "busy" work that you have been doing up to this point.

- Bargain with yourself and reward yourself when you succeed and complete your planned intentional behavior. Sample self-promises might be "I will spend some time on social media after I have studied for my exam for two 40-minute blocks," or "I will enjoy some time off and go see a movie once I have completed a 45-minute focused session of high energy action each day this week." Your parents bargain with you all the time, so learn from them and start bargaining with yourself!

HACK #21

Start Today!

It's time to take action and START working on that thing that you are wanting to achieve! This might seem like a no-brainer, given that we have talked about your mindset, your physical environment, your health and wellbeing, your time management, your attitude, your ways of accelerating and taking action towards finally *doing* that thing that you have set as your goal, dream or desire…

HOWEVER!

I know that there will be some people who read this book, as well as every other mindset or time-management or motivation book out there, who are *still* yet to actually put pen to paper or paint to canvas, or lift a weight or write a song.

If you are one of these people, or if you simply find yourself still dragging your feet in self-doubt after reading all of the previous 20 hacks, it's time to ask yourself some hard questions:

"Do I *really* want to achieve this goal?"

"What would it *feel* like to achieve this goal?"

"Do I *really* want to create a life that *rocks*?"

"What would it *feel and look* like in one, three or five years' time if I *do* work today towards the life that I want to create?

"What would it *feel* and *look* like if I *don't* work towards the life that I want to create?"

"If I were told that I only had months to live, would I feel that I had *lived my life to the fullest*?"

What *would* it feel like if you didn't achieve your goal?

If the pain of not achieving that goal feels awful, you have your answer right there.

It's time to harden up, soldier.

Sit your butt down at your computer, or at the gym, or in front of your school books, or at your instrument, easel or writing journal! Wherever your butt needs to be, get it there and take *intentional*, high energy, focused action *today*!

Do you remember being a kid and discovering that not everything in life is fun? Your parents made you eat vegetables instead of just icecream. You were told to get outside and run around instead of being allowed to spend your entire weekend on your Xbox. As you hit high school you were told that study and hard work are necessary to help you get the grades you need to go into the career that you want.

The thing is, generally speaking, you did what you were told, because if you didn't you wouldn't know how to tie your shoe laces or boil an egg or read and write. Unfortunately though, when it comes to creating the life that you want, your parents and teachers are not going to be there every step of the way to tell you what to do next and punish or reward you along the way. Motivation, planning and choosing to work hard is totally your call now.

It's up to you to choose if you want to binge watch Netflix for 5 hours straight or tackle that essay.

"I'm too busy chatting to my friends."

"I'm just not in the mood today."

"I'm not feeling inspired to write."

"The planets didn't align."

Excuses are limitless and get more and more creative when we procrastinate instead of actually *doing* the things that we need to do to create the life that we want!

One of the lines that I was known for as a personal trainer was "Suck it up, princess!" I used it when my clients were moaning about doing burpees or push-ups. My job as their trainer was to push these men and women further than they would have pushed themselves, and there were satisfied smiles at the end of the session every time – not just because they survived (*grin*), but because they achieved what they had thought was impossible.

It's now time to become your own personal trainer, holding yourself accountable and accepting no excuses when you know that you are trying to dodge hard work.

It's time for you to suck it up, princess!

The side of you that wants instant gratification will always want to avoid hard or uncomfortable work. You'll suddenly find that you want to raid the fridge, scroll through Facebook or flick through Netflix whenever it is time to focus on hard tasks. These are the times when you need to discipline yourself to ignore those urges and instead choose to take the right action.

I used to tell my gym clients that if they could push through those painful first 5–10 minutes of exercise, then the endorphins, or happy hormones, would start to kick in and the process would get easier. Not easier in regards to what they had to do, but easier in their inner fight against it. I've found this same mind game works for myself, whether I am in the gym, practicing my instrument or sitting down to write. If I can push through all of my excuses, my feelings and my sheer laziness, and simply *start*, within 5–10 minutes my resistance begins to melt away and I find myself getting on with the task that is going to help me create the *rocking* life that I want.

Isn't it ironic that we procrastinate and stuff around

instead of taking action and doing the tasks that will help us get closer to achieving the dream that we have? For some people, that inner resistance can cause them to stuff up their goal completely – but not you. This time is different, isn't it?

How many people have said that they would love to write a book? A much larger number compared to those who actually start. And there are far more who start than who actually finish.

It's crunch time now.

Do you want to be the person who *talks* about the dream that they once had, or do you want to be the person who *achieves* that dream?

Do you want to live with the regret of never even *starting* the process of working towards your dream, or do you want to experience the thrill of *doing* that thing you are wanting to do?

Do you want to live the life that *you* created, or do you just want be one of those people that talks about all the things that they were *going* to do, but never actually did?

What action are you going to take today to actually *start*?

ACTION TASKS:

- Identify what action you need to take to start working towards your goal. Is it to plan your book structure, visit a gym for a walk-through, book an art class, map out your assignment and study schedule, or talk to someone about a job?
- Schedule the times that you are going to do these tasks into your planner, including one for TODAY!
- Let someone in your dream team know that you are starting your project today, then take it one step further and let them know that you are going to check in with them once a week to let them know how many hours you have done.
- Put down this book and start TODAY!

A FINAL WORD FROM CAT

I believe in you.

Really!

If you have made it this far through the book, that shows me that you are not someone who is wanting to settle for a second-best life. No, you are someone who is honest and real about wanting to create a life that *rocks*!

You are someone who is brave enough and maybe crazy enough to believe that you exist for a purpose that is bigger than just yourself. You've reached the stage where you don't want to simply float along, letting life just happen – you are ready to take responsibility and *create* the life that you want!

There is no special magic that causes some people to work towards their goals with laser focus while others with similar goals can't seem to get started. In the same way, none of the hacks I have listed here are rocket science; however, I can guarantee that the people who are actually *doing* the work that they set out to do have used many of them during their journey.

If you commit to reading these 21 hacks and actually *doing* the action steps I have given you, I can guarantee that your life will not be the same in a month's time. You will feel motivated, positive, confident, in control, focused, full of self-belief and not just *hoping* to rock your life – but actually *doing* it!

You see, there is a secret I have been holding all through this book until this last section. Living a life that *rocks* is not something that you "arrive at" one day. It is something that you do *every day* as you journey through life. If you know that you have a purpose to live for, e.g: to help people or animals, to perform on a stage or to create a business that changes lives – and you live your life so that you are taking action *every day* towards fulfilling that purpose, then you are truly *rocking* your life!

Even if you are still in school!

People who live their lives like this are the people who change the world – because they impact and change their communities while they do that thing that they are uniquely called to do. Imagine what a difference it would make in the world if the 14, 17, 19 year olds started living that way now, taking charge of their lives and working towards their dreams!

Isn't it time that you joined them?

Isn't it time that you created the roadmap for your life?

Isn't it time that you chose to live a life that *rocks*?

You've got a tool box of practical hacks to help you get going, so start today. And, guess what, if you decide next year that your dream is actually different to what you thought, you simply change direction. All of the effort you will have made won't be wasted. You will have strengthened your will-power muscle, learned self-discipline from applying the hacks and will be able to transfer this experience towards your new path.

Again – I believe in you, and I would love to hear how taking action with these 21 hacks has helped you *rock your life* and impacted those around you!

Cat x
Auckland, 2020

ACKNOWLEDGEMENTS

As always, my first acknowledgement goes to the man who always has my back, my husband Leli. Whilst your coffee slurping habit will continue to irritate me until the day I die, you are an amazing man to whom I am enormously grateful. I am especially thankful that you didn't move out when I brought that third cat home.

I am surrounded by amazing women who continually inspire, encourage and motivate me. You all know who you are and you ladies seriously *rock!* Special mentions go to Pauline Stockhaussen, Jayne Albiston, Kiri Maree Moore, Kirsty Salisbury and Cat Levine who have all seen me at my lowest and still hung in there with me.

To the team at Indie Experts who have believed in me from the get go, thank you so much for your guidance and encouragement. Ann and Dixie, it is so wonderful being on this journey together.

Finally, a big shout out to James Altucher all the way across the ditch in the Big Apple. You threw out a writing prompt that literally changed my life down here in New Zealand. I've been a fan-girl of your writing for ages and fingers crossed that I can shake your hand and say thank you to your face one day!

Finally, if you have read this far – thank you to you for believing in yourself enough to read *21 Hacks to ROCK your Life*! Get out there, make your dreams a reality and create a positive impact in the world.

You've got this!

ABOUT CAT COLUCCIO

Cat Coluccio is an Author, a Reinvention Coach, the host of the **Rocking Midlife® Podcast** and **Community** – *and a champion of midlife women.*

A qualified Educator, Personal Trainer and Life Coach, Cat is passionate about seeing women empowered to stop procrastinating, identify their values and goals, take intentional action and build purposeful lives and businesses, creating a legacy for their families and communities.

At home speaking on both live or virtual stages, Cat has been a featured guest on numerous international podcasts and summits, as well as in national print publications, television and radio shows.

A transplanted Australian, Cat resides in New Zealand with her husband, children and grandson, along with far too many cats, chooks and sheep. She's partial to a glass of prosecco and a laugh with friends, good chocolate, great books, and lives by her personal philosophy: *"It's never too late to have a new beginning in life."*

WANT MORE CAT?

Check out Cat's other 21 Hacks books!

21 Hacks to ROCK your Life!
*Stop Procrastinating, Do that Thing
and Live a Life ON-Purpose!*

21 Hacks to ROCK your Midlife!
Release the Past, Dare to Dream and Create your Legacy!

Find these titles and more by following
Cat's author page HERE: https://amzn.to/3A2XoKu

Want more FREE resources to help you ROCK your life?

Check out Cat's website HERE: www.catcoluccio.com

Let's get Social!

F: @catcoluccio
IG: @catcoluccio
Pin: @catcoluccio
YT: @catcoluccio

Want some cool clothing, gifts and motivating printables?

Check out Cat's 2 ETSY shops HERE:

Rocking Midlife®:
https://www.etsy.com/nz/shop/rockingmidlife

Rock your Side-Hustle:
https://www.etsy.com/nz/shop/RockyourSideHustle

ENDNOTES

1 Sheard, M., & Golby, J. (2006). Effect of a Psychological Skills Training Programme on Swimming Performance and Positive Psychological Development. International Journal of Sport and Exercise Psychology, 4, 149–169.

2 Peters, Madelon M L et al. "Manipulating optimism: Can imagining a best possible self be used to increase positive future expectancies?" (2010).

3 Ajala, Emmanuel Majekodunmi. "THE INFLUENCE OF WORKPLACE ENVIRONMENT ON WORKERS' WELFARE, PERFORMANCE AND PRODUCTIVITY." (2012).

4 T Bernstein, Ethan and Stephen Turban. "The impact of the 'open' workspace on human collaboration." *Philosophical transactions of the Royal Society of London. Series B, Biological sciences* (2018).

5 Clark, Charlotte et al. "Exposure-effect relations between aircraft and road traffic noise exposure at school and reading comprehension: the RANCH project." *American journal of epidemiology* 163 1 (2006): 27–37.

6 CEO The Sound Agency https://resonics.co.uk/12-ways-noise-affects-employee-wellbeing-health-productivity/

7 Padmanabhan, Rajiv et al. "A prospective, randomised, controlled study examining binaural beat audio and pre-operative anxiety

in patients undergoing general anaesthesia for day case surgery." *Anaesthesia* 60 9 (2005): 874–7.

8   https://thriveglobal.com/stories/these-7-tips-will-help-you-sleep-better-backed-by-science/

9   Chellappa, Sarah L. et al. "Acute exposure to evening blue-enriched light impacts on human sleep." *Journal of sleep research* 22 5 (2013): 573–80.

10 Obradovich, Nick et al. "Nighttime temperature and human sleep loss in a changing climate." *Science Advances* (2017).

11 Panza, Francesco et al. "Contribution of Mediterranean Diet in the Prevention of Alzheimer's Disease." (2018).

12 "Nutrient Reference Values for Australia and New Zealand" www.moh.govt.nz

13 Willis, Lauren M. et al. "Modulation of cognition and behavior in aged animals: role for antioxidant- and essential fatty acid-rich plant foods." *The American journal of clinical nutrition* 89 5 (2009): 1602S–1606S.

14 Masento, Natalie et al. "Effects of hydration status on cognitive performance and mood." *The British journal of nutrition* 111 10 (2014): 1841–52.

15 Claessens, Bjc Brigitte et al. "A review of the time management literature." (2007).

16 Cirillo, Francesco. "The Pomodoro Technique: The Life-Changing Time-Management System." (2018).

17 Klassen, Robert M. et al. "Academic procrastination of under-graduates: Low self-efficacy to self-regulate predicts higher levels of procrastination." (2008).

18 Ibid.

19 Malik, Maria Ashraf. "The Relationship between Myers Briggs Type Indicator (MBTI) and Emotional Intelligence among University Students." (2014).

REFERENCES

Ajala, Emmanuel Majekodunmi. "The Influence of Workplace Environment on Workers' Welfare, Performance and Productivity." (2012).

Banbury, Simon P. and Dianne C. Berry. "Disruption of office-related tasks by speech and office noise." (1998).

Chellappa, Sarah L. et al. "Acute exposure to evening blue-enriched light impacts on human sleep." *Journal of sleep research* 22 5 (2013): 573–80.

Cirillo, Francesco. "The Pomodoro Technique: The Life-Changing Time-Management System." (2018)

Claessens, Bjc Brigitte et al. "A review of the time management literature." (2007).

Clark, Charlotte et al. "Exposure-effect relations between aircraft and road traffic noise exposure at school and reading comprehension: the RANCH project." *American journal of epidemiology* 163 1 (2006): 27–37.

Costa, Arthur L. and Bena Kallick. "Learning and Leading with Habits of Mind: 16 Essential Characteristics for Success." (2009).

Harvard Health: https://www.health.harvard.edu/staying-healthy/5-of-the-best-exercises-you-can-ever-do

Jon Kabat-Zinn: https://www.umassmed.edu/cfm/about-us/people/2-meet-our-faculty/kabat-zinn-profile/

Klassen, Robert M. et al. "Academic procrastination of undergraduates: Low self-efficacy to self-regulate predicts higher levels of procrastination." (2008).

Loh, KepKee et al. "Higher Media Multi-Tasking Activity Is Associated with Smaller Gray-Matter Density in the Anterior Cingulate Cortex." *PloS one* (2014).

Malik, Maria Ashraf. "The Relationship between Myers Briggs Type Indicator (MBTI) and Emotional Intelligence among University Students." (2014).

Masento, Natalie et al. "Effects of hydration status on cognitive performance and mood." *The British journal of nutrition* 111 10 (2014): 1841–52.

Ministry of Health NZ: www.moh.govt.nz

Obradovich, Nick et al. "Nighttime temperature and human sleep loss in a changing climate." *Science Advances* (2017).

Padmanabhan, Rajiv et al. "A prospective, randomised, controlled study examining binaural beat audio and pre-operative anxiety in patients undergoing general anaesthesia for day case surgery." *Anaesthesia* 60 9 (2005): 874–7.

Panza, Francesco et al. "Contribution of Mediterranean Diet in the Prevention of Alzheimer's Disease." (2018).

Peters, Madelon M L et al. "Manipulating optimism: Can imagining a best possible self be used to increase positive future expectancies?" (2010).

Resonics: CEO The Sound Agency https://resonics.co.uk/12-ways-noise-affects-employee-wellbeing-health-productivity/

Sheard, M., & Golby, J. (2006). Effect of a Psychological Skills Training Programme on Swimming Performance and Positive Psychological Development. International Journal of Sport and Exercise Psychology, 4, 149–169.

T Bernstein, Ethan and Stephen Turban. "The impact of the 'open' workspace on human collaboration." *Philosophical transactions of the Royal Society of London. Series B, Biological sciences* (2018).

Thrive Global: https://thriveglobal.com/stories/these-7-tips-will-help-you-sleep-better-backed-by-science/

Willis, Lauren M. et al. "Modulation of cognition and behavior in aged animals: role for antioxidant- and essential fatty acid-rich plant foods." *The American journal of clinical nutrition* 89 5 (2009): 1602S-1606S.

www.ingramcontent.com/pod-product-compliance
Lightning Source LLC
Chambersburg PA
CBHW050314010526
44107CB00055B/2234